The Comparative Study of Local Government and Politics

The World of Political Science— The development of the discipline

Book series edited by Michael Stein and John Trent

Professors **Michael B. Stein** and **John E. Trent** are the co-editors of the book series "The World of Political Science". The former is professor of Political Science at McMaster University in Hamilton, Ontario, Canada. The latter is a Fellow in the Center of Governance of the University of Ottawa, in Ottawa, Ontario, Canada, and a former professor in its Department of Political science.
Dr.**Tim Heinmiller** is the coordinator of the series, and Assistant Professor of Political Science at Brock University in St. Catherines, Ontario, Canada.

Harald Baldersheim
Hellmut Wollmann (eds.)

The Comparative Study of Local Government and Politics
Overview and Synthesis

Barbara Budrich Publishers
Opladen & Farmington Hills 2006

A CIP catalogue record for this book is available from
Die Deutsche Bibliothek (The German Library)

© 2006 by Barbara Budrich Publishers, Opladen
www.barbara-budrich.net

ISBN 10   3-86649-034-8 (paperback)
ISBN 13   978-3-86649-034-5

Das Werk einschließlich aller seiner Teile ist urheberrechtlich geschützt. Jede Verwertung außerhalb der engen Grenzen des Urheberrechtsgesetzes ist ohne Zustimmung des Verlages unzulässig und strafbar. Das gilt insbesondere für Vervielfältigungen, Übersetzungen, Mikroverfilmungen und die Einspeicherung und Verarbeitung in elektronischen Systemen.

Die Deutsche Bibliothek – CIP-Einheitsaufnahme
Ein Titeldatensatz für die Publikation ist bei Der Deutschen Bibliothek erhältlich.

Verlag Barbara Budrich ⓑ Barbara Budrich Publishers
Stauffenbergstr. 7. D-51379 Leverkusen Opladen, Germany

28347 Ridgebrook. Farmington Hills, MI 48334. USA
www.barbara-budrich.net

Jacket illustration by disegno, Wuppertal, Germany – www.disenjo.de
Typesetting: Susanne Rosenkranz, Opladen, Germany
Printed in Europe on acid-free paper by
Paper & Tinta, Poland

Contents

Series Editors' Preface

This is the fifth volume in our new book series entitled "The World of Political Science" sponsored by the Research Committee on the Study of Political Science as a Discipline (RC 33), one of about 50 Research Committees of the International Political Science Association (IPSA). Each volume of the series is being prepared by leading international scholars representing one of the research committees of IPSA. We expect to publish up to 20 volumes in the series over the next three years.

"The World of Political Science" series is intended to fulfil several objectives. First, it is international in scope, and includes contributors from all corners of the globe. Second, it aims to provide an up-to-date overview of a specific sub-field of political science. Third, although prepared by leading academic specialists, it is written in a manner which is meant to be accessible both to students of that field and also those who want to learn more about it. Fourth, the books offer both a state-of-the-art overview of the sub-field and an explanation of how it has evolved into what it is today. Thus it serves as part of a broader objective of evaluating the current state of development of political science. Fifth, on the basis of this evaluation, the volume editors and authors will make proposals for the improvement of each sub-field and eventually, for the discipline as a whole.

Local Government and Politics is not the subject that is at the forefront of everyone's mind when they think of political science. And yet "town hall politics" are the bedrock of political systems. One might well say that as municipalities go, so goes modern democracy. That is why the rigorous study of local government and politics is so important to our discipline. Local government practitioners will find the research about their institutions in this volume to be encyclopedic and yet painstakingly thorough. As well as being learned, it is also concise and informative. Students and professors will be rewarded by the originality of the unique chapters on the political science research methods and academic infrastructure. But the authors and editors are also at pains to point out such weaknesses as the lack of international taxonomies, the dearth of understanding of all the implications new political innovations for municipal government, and the relatively little information about developing countries. In other words, this book is what a state-of-the-art survey should be: highly informative about the evolution of local government and the research on it as well as establishing the paths on which political science should move ahead.

We want to express our profound appreciation to the editors of the volume, Harald Baldersheim and Hellmut Wollmann for their strong leadership and determination in rapidly producing this volume. Thanks also to the authors of IPSA Research Committee 05 on Local Government and Politics for their notable contributions. We also want to thank our publisher, Barbara Budrich, whose vision and determination as publisher are largely responsible for bringing the series to fruition. We also acknowledge our deep gratitude to the Social Science and Humanities Research Council of Canada (SSHRC), whose initial Research Development Initiatives Grant #820-1999-1022 and later extensions made the project possible. In addition, we gratefully acknowledge the work of IPSA Research Committee 33 on the Study of Political Science as a Discipline and its Project Sub-Committee members, as well as the support given by the IPSA Committee on Research and Training (CRT). Finally, a special word of thanks is owed to our Project Coordinator, Tim Heinmiller, who applied his considerable academic and administrative capabilities to all major concerns of this volume.

Of course, ultimate responsibility for the series belongs to us, the co-editors. This project has been a joint and equal collaborative effort on our part right from its beginning, and we are very pleased to see this effort finally come to fruition.

John Trent (University of Ottawa)
Michael Stein (McMaster University)

Preface

In the year 2000 the Research Committee 33 (RC 33) of the *International Political Science Association* (IPSA) presented the idea that the Research Committees of IPSA should undertake a collective effort, each in its respective sub-field, to give an overview and account of its current development and the prevailing research paradigms of the sub-field. While making it a point, in an early guideline, that the books emerging from such efforts should "not simply be another 'state of the art' exercise", a template was proposed which was meant to make sure that a set of information (on the "infrastructure", methods, key issues, main research and discourse traditions and crucial perspectives) be presented in each of the proposed volumes, thus making the accounts somewhat comparative and their results (hopefully) sources of cross-feritilisation across the different Research Committees and their sub-fields. The underlying (and laudable) idea of this initiative, undertaken by RC 33 and further promoted by *John Trent, Michael Stein* and *Tim Heinmiller,* obviously is to encourage the publication of a series of volumes which, under the general heading of "the world of political science". The ensuing volumes should, for one, stimulate and synthesise discourse and exchange *within* the respective "sub-disciplinary" fields (often enough falling into deplorably fragmented "sub-sub-disciplines") and should, furthermore, enlarge and mutually enrich the discourse and exchange within the wider discipline and "world of political science", and even beyond, to attract the attention and interest of a larger audience and readership, not least among the practitioners. In this understanding and reading, the book series revolving around the "world of political science" is a very ambitious one, indeed.

Members of the IPSA Research Committee 05 (RC 05) (*"on the comparative study of local government and politics"*) have responded to this opportunity. The volume which is hereby presented is the result of the collective effort of RC 05 members.

In view of the wide topical range and reach following from the template meant to guide the volumes of this book series, the articles presented in this book are bound to selective, given the limited space available for the reviews of the respective topics to be covered. No doubt, the internationally available literature on local government is marked by some "Western-world" bias, maybe also an Anglo-Saxon centricity, accentuated by the dominance of the English/American language as lingua franca in international scholarly exchange. Although the list of authors of this volume may seem to reproduce this somewhat biased regional representation, a deliberate attempt was made to keep the conceptual and empirical and horizon wide open in order to overcome such "centricities".

Such literally world-wide openness and representation has, we are confident to say, imbued the activities of the RC 05 which, it should be added at this point, is among the Research Committees first established by IPSA, as it was founded in the early 1970s. Throughout its history it has sought to be an open forum for research and debate on local government developments in all parts of the worlds. After 1989 the Committee was focussed especially on the dramatic transformations taking place after the fall of the Berlin Wall, which gave scholars in the field of local government studies an opportunity to be observers, almost literally, of the birth of local democracy in previously communist countries.

At this point another note of "self-advertisement" may be permitted. Four years ago, in association with RC 05, an English-language book series was initiated by members of RC which, in accordance with the RC's regionally wide scope and open mandate, comprise volumes of global reach as well as books more specifically on post-communist countries as well as South East Asia and European countries.

In conclusion we wish to thank the IPSA colleagues involved in editing the IPSA series "World of Political Science", that is, John Trent, Michael Stein and Tim Heinmiller, for their support (and also patience) for the publication of this volume.

May the volume find critically interested (and numerous) readers inside and outside local government research

Berlin and Oslo, June 2006

Harald Baldersheim   *Hellmut Wollmann*

Chapter 1
From Community to Power and Back Again?

Michael Goldsmith

Introduction

This essay reviews the contribution made to the study of urban politics and local government by political scientists over the last forty years. It covers a wide range of topics, including the old community power debate and its later variant regime theory, via a concern with metropolitan government and politics; output studies and fiscal stress; intergovernmental relations; social capital, as well as the impact of the EU on local government and the emergence of the meso level. It concludes by considering some research topics which merit further attention and research. Any such survey inevitably reflects personal experience and interests: in this case it reflects the author's journey through a territory that has stimulated his interest for more than forty years. And since the original request was to consider the contribution of European political scientists, much of the essay has this focus.

Most of this essay is structured around that forty-year perspective, since each decade has brought with it its own particular focus or contribution to developments within the area and to the discipline more generally. But at the outset one must place on record the immense and important contribution made by US scholars to the field. Most of the innovations, together with substantial contributions to theory as well as substantive empirical studies, have been made in this field by American scholars, as has been the case with most other sub-fields in political science since the Second World War. This contribution reflects the numerical superiority of American political science as compared with its European and other counterparts, as reflected in membership of, and attendance at national association annual gatherings, and by the range of specialist groups and journals available under the US umbrella as compared to the European counterparts. It also reflects the relatively more generous research funding available to US scholars, especially at particular times over the last forty years. For example, in the 1950s and 1960s, when much important and well-funded work was undertaken by US political scientists, social science research funding was generally in its infancy in most European countries – indeed as was the discipline itself, with many European political scientists learning their trade by doing graduate work in the United States. In this context it is important to recognise the contribution to our understanding of democracy and participation, and to ideas about civic values, by such scholars as Dahl (1963), Almond and Verba (1963), the contribution made to the development of policy analysis and our understanding of outputs and outcomes by writers such as Dye (1966), Hofferbert (1975) and Sharkansky (1970). In all these cases, the methodological and empirical contributions were considerable. More recently the US contribution has been more specific, but no less important – one might, for example, highlight Sassen's work on globalization (Sassen: 1991; 1994); Putnam on social capital (1993; 2000); Clark on new political culture (1998) and Stone (1989) on urban regimes.

1960s 1: Community power

Like many researchers of his generation, this author was attracted to the local government/ urban politics field by the work of Dahl (1961) and Hunter (1953) and the community power debate in the US of the late fifties and early sixties, with the interest further stimulated by the work of Edward Banfield.[1] The attraction was that these books seemed to analyse city politics as they were, rather than the dreary descriptive accounts available about local government in Britain at the time, or the more normative work similarly produced then. The community power debate raged for over a decade in the American literature, with literally thousands of communities, municipalities and cities being subject to empirical study using variants on Hunter's original elitist or Dahl's pluralist approaches. Inevitably the conclusion was that in most cases power was in the hands of elites, generally of higher economic and social class than the population as a whole, but rarely did a single elite control all aspects of decision making. Yet there was little doubt that there was a mobilisation of bias, to use Schattsneider's (1960) phrase[2], in favour of major economic interests, with policies favouring growth and development rather than redistribution. Overall, the contribution made was to our understanding of power and how it is used, can be measured and studied at the local level.

Yet in practice few European scholars (and they were largely British ones at that time) followed down a similar route.[3] In part this was a reflection of the fact that many Northern European states had extensive welfare provision, often delegated by the national level to local governments for implementation. In part it was also true to say that most European local governments did not have economic development/regeneration high on their agenda at the time – and

---

1   Hunter F (1953); Dahl R.A. (1961); Banfield E C and Wilson J (1963).
2   The phrase is from Schattschneider E E (1960): The Semi-Sovereign People, New York, Holt, Rhinehart and Winston.
3   The exceptions were the work undertaken by Saunders on Croydon and Green on Bath, some of which was reported in Saunders (1975; 1980) and Green (1967)

again it was perhaps national governments who were seen as being responsible for economic health and growth rather than localities. It was also a reflection of the highly partisan nature of most European local government (North and South), another contrast with its North American counterpart where, in both the United States and Canada, a tradition of non-partisan local government emerged in the post first world war period as part of the reform movement. Party political elites dominated local politics far more in Europe than was the case in North America, with the result that local politics were more accessible to a wider social base than was the case in some parts of North America. (Lee: 1963). To study only local elections, parties and their role in elite recruitment locally was largely believed to answer the question of who governs?[4] Thus, for example, taking Young's (1975) collection as a guide to what interested mainly British scholars at the time, we find pieces by Stanyer on local elections; Newton on lessons from the community power debate, or Young on metropolitan integration.

1960s 2: Local government Reform

If community power was less of a research question in the UK than it might or indeed should have been (Dunleavy: 1980), other questions dominated the agenda. Most important were issues surrounding metropolitan government and the reform of institutional structures generally, both in terms of official reports and more academic research. From the sixties onwards, reform of the institutional structure of local government was on the agenda of many European states, especially in northern Europe, with countries like Britain, Denmark, Norway, Sweden and the Netherlands undertaking a variety of reforms of structure and organization.[5] Whilst the US showed some concern with the reform of (particularly metropolitan) government in the sixties, it was never seriously on either the political or academic agenda.[6] The exception was the United States' neighbour to the North, where reform of metropolitan government was extensive during the sixties and seventies.[7] But the reform of local government in Britain and elsewhere in Europe attracted considerable attention by researchers, both European and North American. Thus, for example London reform was researched by scholars such as Smallwood (1965) and

---

4   See for example Bulpitt (1967); Hampton (1970; Jones (1969); Newton (1969; 1976). On
      voting see Sharpe (ed.) (1967) and Stanyer (1975).
5   Reforms included Britain (London – 1966; the rest 1972); Denmark (1971); Norway and
      Sweden (1973), the Netherlands (1970). For a discussion of these and other reforms see
      Gunlicks (1981).
6   See for example Danielson M N (1971).
7   For a discussion see inter alia Kaplan H (1982).

Rhodes (1970); the later reforms by people like Wood (1976) and Dearlove (1979), whilst Gustafsson (1981) examined Sweden; Leemans, (1972) and Morlan (1981) examined the Netherlands. A comparative assessment of these reforms can be found in Dente and Kjellberg (1988). Overall, much of this work suggested that the reform of local institutions, particularly in terms of either undertaking some form of municipal amalgamation or of introducing some form of metropolitan government was, with a few notable exceptions, easier in Northern Europe than in the South, where small municipalites, with few functional responsibilities remained the norm. However, it might be true to say that Mitterand's 1981 decentralization reforms in France, a series of reforms in Spain and Italy have made the North –South distinction slightly less valid today. Even if there are still 36000 communes in France, decentralization has led to considerable collaboration amongst communes – the so-called Community of Communes and more recently to reforms at the metropolitan level, albeit largely of a voluntary nature and with greater or lesser degrees of success.[8] Generally speaking one has seen a strengthening of what Sharpe (1993) called the meso or intermediate tier of government as a result of a continuing process of decentralization and deconcentration across Europe as a whole, though one has to agree with Keating's (1998) assessment that much of territorial politics in Europe is in a state of flux.

1970s 1: Outputs or
What Difference Does it Make Who Governs?

The late sixties and early seventies in the United States in this field saw the emergence of what came to be known as output studies, designed largely to answer the question in this section's title. American work by Dye (1966), Hofferbert (1975) and Sharkansky (1970) amongst others highlighted the extent to which economic variables seemed to determine policy, rather than the actions of politicians. This work stimulated some (largely British) research, where expectations were that politics mattered rather more than the American work suggested. In the event early work was equivocal in providing an answer (Davies: 1968, 1975); Boaden: (1971); Nicholson and Topham (1971), Danziger (1979), and a fuller answer had to wait for the publication of extensive research undertaken by Sharpe and Newton (1977, 1984). Part of the problem with much of this outputs work lay in its theoretical foundations – largely determined by Eastonian systems analysis – (as Dearlove (1979: 75) so aptly noted, the world is not made up of little black boxes) and by the tendency for the researcher with 'the biggest deck of

---

8   An interesting comparative contribution is that of Kjellberg and Hoffmann-Martinot (1996).

punched cards' to 'win' the current debates! For a critical review I refer to Boyne's (1985) seminal article, whilst his own work in this area repays further study. Work of this kind attracted little attention elsewhere is Europe (one exception is the work of Mouritzen: 1991), and the question of why policies and their impacts differ remains one to which research attention could usefully be given again – a point to which we shall return later.

1970s 2: The Marxist contribution

As one surveys the movement of ideas in the social sciences back and forth across the Atlantic, one is struck by a fact that implicitly has already been recognized – namely that much of the traffic has largely been one way since the early fifties, whether one is looking at areas like election studies; political culture and the urban politics field, albeit with some inevitable time lag. In the latter case the exception was the impact of Marxist urban contributions from the mid seventies onwards, as French and other work was translated into English, (see for example Pickvance: 1976), most notably that of people like Castells (1975; 1979) and Lojkine (1976). In this area, ideas about collective consumption and urban social movements – especially concerning the power of the latter to bring about change at the local level and how collective consumption could help to modify the worse excesses of capitalism. British writers who took up this work included Saunders (1975; 1979; 1986); Dunleavy (1980) and Gurr and King (1987). Pickvance (1995) provides an excellent review of the field. A third theme was raised by critical German writers such as Habermas (1976) and Offe (1976, 1984), especially on issues of legitimacy. Whilst this work was to be put on the back burner by the events of 1989 and after in central and east Europe, it still helps to shape discussions on important questions such as globalization and its urban impacts, another question to which we shall return. The power of this writing was so strong that for a number of years in the eighties it forced North American political scientists to address some of the issues it raised, and I think changed the shape of the urban politics literature for some time. United States writers who particularly responded to this approach included the Fainsteins (1986); Mollenkopf (1983), Smith (1988), and Katznelson (1992).

In many ways the late seventies through to the early nineties was the heyday of European interest in urban politics and local government, with other disciplines such as sociology, geography; planning and even history making important contributions to European debates.[9] Cross disciplinary gatherings

---

9   See for example the contribution of geographers like David Harvey, sociologists such as Lojkine, Pickvance and Saunders, and historians such as Fraser and Hennock.

were common in Britain, also drawing in European participants; and as the European Consortium for Political Research grew in strength, its workshops provided opportunities for European wide debate. IPSA, through the work of the IPSA Research Committee on Local Government led initially by the late Franco Kjellberg, subsequently by Helmut Wollman and Harald Baldersheim, also stimulated exchanges. Comparative work, especially amongst Europeans, was also beginning.

One important theme in this period, partly produced out of people's experience of the large scale welfare provision and the part played by local governments in its provision, which emerged at this time (mid-seventies) was the question of what Pahl (1975) referred to as urban managerialism. The reference is to the role of professional bureaucrats in determining policy and its impacts, particularly important again in Northern Europe where considerable professional expertise is located in bureaucrats at the local level. Another theme – drawing particularly on French experience and which was related to the expertise theme – lay in the studies of inter-organisational relationships by writers such as Gremion (1976); Crozier (1964), with Thoenig (1976) and in Germany by Scharpf (1978). This latter work was to provide an important stimulus to the early eighties, not only in Britain but elsewhere, on intergovernmental relations. This period also saw the first flowering of European (with some North American involvement it must be admitted) co-operation, when writers like Kjellberg, Hansen, Bruun, Dente, Sharpe, Simienska and Wiatr all contributed to the International Political Sciences Review (IPSR) special issue on recent changes in urban politics (IPSR, vol 1 no 2 1980).

The transatlantic flow was reversed – or at least slowed – by the experience of a number of US cities with bankruptcy in the late seventies and early eighties. Clark's work (Clark and Ferguson: 1983) on fiscal crisis aroused considerable interest in Europe, and ECPR Workshops saw important work emerging – again by Sharpe (1981) and Newton (1980). This work was not without some difficulty – whilst American cities could go bottom up, by contrast in many European countries local governments were effectively creatures of the state, which also guaranteed or underwrote their debts. Furthermore, as Mouritzen (1992) was to demonstrate, many European countries were relatively wealthy, so that local governments, rather than facing fiscal stress, were suffering from the opposite – a kind of fiscal gain, as central governments were able to finance the ever-increasing cost of rising public services delivered at the local level. It was not until the emergence of the Thatcher government in Britain in the eighties, and to economic downturn in some other parts of Europe (notably Finland, Sweden and to a lesser extent Denmark in the late eighties/early nineties), that European local governments and their national counterparts began to feel the stress associated with rising expectations of public services on the one hand and of changing demographics (especially ageing, healthier but generally static populations). Today increasingly the rising cost of the HEW (health, education and welfare) functions poses problems for governments in most countries. But European local governments have never faced anything like the fiscal stress experienced by cities like Cleveland and New York in the 1970s. In Britain the best example was Liverpool in the mid eighties, (Parkinson: 1986) whilst Sweden and Finland in the nineties saw drastic cutbacks and some re-organization of service provision (Lane: 1997). It was the emergence of neo-liberal governments at the national level in countries such as Britain and Sweden, intent on rolling back the state that generated the crisis. For example, work by Stoker (1991); Rhodes (1981; 1986; 1988) and Cochrane (1993) demonstrated the extent of centralization in British politics, together with the way in which local service delivery became fragmented through the eighties, with the consequent loss of status for British local government.

1980s 1: Intergovernmental Relations:

Since the early eighties, Britain in particular, but also mirrored in other European countries, has seen a number of research funding initiatives aimed at local government and urban politics. The early to mid eighties was the period when intergovernmental relations was a focus of attention in many countries. There was decentralization in France under Mitterand in 1981; new experience of local government in Spain and Portugal in the era after Franco and Salazar; reform in Italy, as well as re-structured local government in Scandinavia. In Germany the lander provided a focus of attention on the regional level, which was to grow again in the late eighties and early nineties. But it was probably the British and French cases that attracted the most attention. The then SSRC (later ESRC) initiative on central-local government relations (which this author was fortunate enough to co-ordinate) provided an opportunity to examine a range of themes from a variety of different perspectives and to open up the possibility of wider international research collaboration. The most important contribution was the stress its findings gave to networks and to the relationships between different policy communities, to use Rhodes' phrase (Rhodes: 1981; 1986; 1988). But the initiative also encouraged wider discussion within Europe of Saunders' dual state theory (Saunders: 1979; 1986) – especially in Scandinavia (Villadsen: 1986), and within Britain raised awareness of the importance of the territorial dimension of British politics, especially through the work of people like Bulpitt (1983) and Rose (1983). It also provided the stimulus for more comparative work in Europe, resulting in such studies as those of Hanf and Scharpf (1978); Page and Goldsmith, (1987); Page (1991); Goldsmith (1995; 2004; 2005)

Preteceille and Pickvance (1991). This British research initiative was followed by one on inner cities, itself followed by the next important development – the research initiative on local governance, co-ordinated by Gerry Stoker, whose work, like that of Jim Sharpe, Ken Newton and Rod Rhodes before him, provided an important developmental push, strongly suggesting the importance of networks, coordination and partnerships between state insitutions and other sectors in successful policy making and implementation.[10]

1990s 1: Governance

As with the earlier decades, the 1990s work in Europe on local government and urban politics reflected two major themes, governance and democratic renewal, both captured in the IPSR special issue of 1998 (Andrews and Goldsmith (eds): IPSR vol 19 no 2), itself somewhat ironically titled *New Trends in Municipal Government* when the major theme is that of governance with the second theme being that of local democracy and democratic renewal. The issue is less focused than its 1980 predecessor, a reflection of the changing research agenda for the sub-area, with articles on politics in divided cities, gender and urban politics, citizenship in Argentinian municipalities alongside those on local governance and theory. A third theme, namely a concern with the spread of ideas generally subsumed under the title of New Public Management, was also a major comparative research interest during this period.

Much 1990s British writing in the field has concentrated on local governance, a reflection first of the increased fragmentation of local political institutions and reduced status enjoyed by British local government in the period since 1979, as well as the results of the major ESRC research initiative on the topic.[11] Whilst it is possible and desirable to argue that the changes in Britain over the last twenty years have placed its local government system almost into the sui generis category (few other countries have gone down such a centralist or fragmented path – possibly New Zealand), undoubtedly some of the changes in Britain have had echoes elsewhere and the governance and new public management agenda has been picked up by writers working on other countries, most notably in France and Scandinavia.[12] What much of this research interestingly reveals is that the increased

---

10 See for example his jointly edited book with Judge and Wolman (1996).

11 The results of which are usefully summarized in Stoker (2000).

12 Much interesting work is being undertaken in France by young urban politics/local government scholars. Mainly available in French, some can be found in English – but in particular work associated with groups working with Balme; LeGalès and Faure. In Scandinavia, new public

fragmentation of local service delivery institutions brought about under the Thatcher/Major regimes, together with an emphasis on new public management ideas, has not really been reversed under the Blair government in Britain – though it has been re-named, whilst elsewhere ideas about New Public Management reflect local interpretations. Again in Britain the large degree of distrust of local government by the centre that research revelaed during the long Conservative years appears to continue under Labour, notwithstanding its apparent commitment to democratic renewal and to devolution (Stoker: 2000; 2004; and Wilson and Game: 2002).

1990s 2: Participation, Local Democracy and Democratic Renewal

The second theme that has occupied European political scientists working in the field has really been that of local democracy. With the increased interest in governance has come a concern that somehow local democracy is not what it was or more particularly is not what it should be. In part this is a reflection of a concern about the numbers voting in local elections; in part a concern with the problems posed by systems of local government in which parties are dominant and the system of representative local democracy somehow does not appear very accountable, in part the way in which local politics may have become more closed as special interests become more dominant, or because – to use Putnam's phrase – social capital is in decline (Putnam: 1993; 2000). But whether it be in countries like Britain (where average turnout in local elections is usually around 40%, but has declined even further in the new century) or whether it be in Norway (where turnout is generally around 70% but declined into the 60% range in the late nineties) governments and voters seem to think that local democracy is somehow under threat or that local politics do not matter: that local government systems somehow do not operate effectively as democratic governments. Perhaps the most important work in this area has been the series of studies undertaken in Norway on local elections and on political participation, many by Rose and Pettersen (1999,2000), though cross national analysis has been undertaken by people like Hoffman-Martinot, Rawlings and Thrasher (1994).

Part of the problem with this debate – which has caught the interest of many junior scholars – is the way in which normative and empirical elements are closely intertwined, so that it becomes easier for normative dispositions to dominate. Thus, for example, individual political participation in local

---

management has attracted attention from people like Ogard in Norway and from Stahlberg and Klaussen – again largely writing in Scandinavian languages.

affairs is seen as a 'good thing.'[13] Furthermore, at least until recently (Stoker and King: 1996; Goldsmith: 1996), our vision of local democracy remained largely trapped in the dogmas of nineteenth century normative philosophy and concerns about representative and responsible government. Re-opening that debate has been an important first step in moving forward, just as have the various European projects on social capital.[14] Both sets of literature are concerned with the basis on which local democracy exists and can develop, as well as the possibilities for 'engineering' improvements through the actions of local governments themselves. But, as Stoker (2004: 121-125) notes, whilst such attempts at engineering democracy (and the United Kingdom, Germany and the Netherlands would provide many examples of such initiative) can make a difference and help enhance individual and group participation in local politics, there is likely to remain a bias in favour of higher status social-economic groups, and such attempts may well be flawed if they are imposed from above rather than built up from below.

The third theme is that of New Public Management, a title which covers a multitude of possible sins. Associated largely with the eighties and the governments of Reagan and Thatcher respectively, New Public Management reforms have their origins in public choice theory and the writings of people like Osborne and Gaebler (1993). Such reforms involve such practices as the privatization and contracting out of public services; the use of agencies to run services, as well as the reform and streamlining of local bureaucracies inter alia. Carried furthest in the United States and Britain, reforms adopted in countries like Germany, Sweden and the Netherlands have often arrived under the New Public Management banner. However, as John (2001: 97) notes, whilst 'New Public Management seems to have a clear set of doctrines, once it is looked at more closely its apparent clarity starts to dissolve and to turn into a set of slogans and contradictory reform programmes.' What is true is that from the seventies onwards, and increasingly since the eighties, public sector management has been undergoing a process of almost continual change. At the centre of this process lies a range of themes abut competition, the reform of hierarchical structures as well as how one can provide incentives to improve performance and to measure it. In this context work by people such as Klaussen and Stahlberg on the Nordic countries, Hendriks and Tops (1999) on the Netherlands and Germany, Wollman and Roth (2000) on

---

13 As a personal example, normatively I am strongly committed to forms of participatory democracy, especially at the local level. Having at various times during my career researched questions of local participation, I know from my empirical work that few people participate in politics and that there is a mobilization of bias toward certain groups. Despite my normative commitment, my empirical research leads me to be rather skeptical about most attempts at 'improving local democracy,' whilst normatively I remain hopeful that they will succeed!

14 See for example the ESRC initiative on Democracy and Participation (details available at http://www.sheff.ac.uk/~pol/Projects/ListofProjects.htm).

Germany, Britain, France and Sweden are representative of comparative work by European scholars in the field.

But the 1990s and the new century have seen a blossoming of other work of interest to students of urban politics and local government in Europe. These different areas of work are not un-related. The first has been to monitor, as far as possible, developments at the local level in central and east Europe after the break up of communism. Particularly important here has been Baldersheim's work (Baldersheim et al.: 1996), whilst Wollman (1999; 2000) has also been active in this area, having also paid attention to change in the former East German territories.

The second theme has been a concern with the impact of globalisation, and most especially Europeanisation, on regional and local governments, especially on the emergence of meso-level or regional governments within the EU member countries. This topic has attracted a lot of attention in the nineties (see inter alia the work of Hooghe: (1996); Keating: (1995, 1997, 1998); Balme (1996); LeGalès and Lequesne (1997); Loughlin (1996); Jeffrey (1997); Goldsmith and Klaussen (1997); Sharpe (1993), some of which continues. The development of the EU, especially post Maastricht with its emphasis on subsidiarity, together with its emphasis from the late eighties onwards on a strong regional policy and on cross border cooperation, has encouraged stronger involvement of the intermediate tier in many policy areas. However, the meso was already strong in Germany through the Lander and the post Franco constitutional settlement in Spain gave important powers and responsibilities to the autonomous communities or regions. If the creation of strong regions in Belgium and Mitterand's decentralisation in France are added in, then EU's regional policy have simply reinforced the further growth of the meso level. Italy, for example, has strengthened the intermediate tier, and even Britain (perhaps the most centralized state in Europe) has moved down the regional road with the devolution of powers to Scotland, Wales and Northern Ireland, as well as the creation of new institutions at the regional level in England.

In this context debate still continues on the relative merits of the regions as compared with cities as actors (see for example LeGalès: 2003) in the context of the new territorial politics of Europe, itself a reflection of the third theme. The eighties and nineties in Western Europe saw localities, especially cities, concerned with their economic performance – particularly in the context of economic regeneration assisted by national and EU levels of government, but also in that of economic competitiveness in the face of globalization. Faced with problems posed by economic restructuring, especially as a result of the decline in primary industries such as steel, textiles and coal, cities and regions have had to adapt their economies. At the same time, as the global economy changes shape, European cities and regions have sought to maintain their position in terms of their competitiveness in the world economy. In this sense, academic concern has not only been to review what cities and regions have done, but also to link this work to that of Stone (1989) and others on regimes.[15] The general conclusion has been that regime theory has perhaps not travelled as well as might be expected (Harding and LeGalès: 1997; Harding: 1995; 2000).

On the whole, urban political scientists, with a few exceptions, have come late to the study of globalization and its impact on urban politics, notwithstanding the pioneering work of Sassen (1991; 1994). Given the multi-dimensional nature of the processes of economic globalization, this late arrival is perhaps not surprising. Much of the work of political scientists has concentrated on the impact of globalization on the role of the nation state, the major exception effectively being the work on the impact of Europeanisation on sub-national governments referred to above, of which the most important development has probably been the introduction of ideas about multi-level governance associated with the work of Marks and Hooghe (1996; 2001).

A third theme – one also with transatlantic connotations – has been a renewed concern with the problems of metropolitan governance, institutions and politics. Such an interest has also arisen in the context of globalization, which has encouraged national and intermediate levels of government to look again on the governance arrangements in major metropolitan areas. Lefevre (1998) provides one of the best comparative reviews, and with others he has undertaken a number of studies across Europe (Jouve and Lefevre: 1999). Also relevant in the European context is the work of Hoffman-Martinot (2000), as well as that led by Heinelt and Kubler (2005). What the research reveals as characteristic of most of the reforms adopted is their largely voluntary cooperative nature (the exceptions being places such as London and Toronto where national and provincial governments have enacted legislation to reform structures), a characteristic these reforms share with developments in the United States (Savitch and Vogel: 1996).

The last development of importance has been the growing amount of comparative work undertaken by Europeans, sometimes in collaboration with their North American counterparts – for example through the Fiscal Austerity and Urban Innovation project (Baldersheim et al.: 1989; Clark and Hoffman-Martinot (1998) or the Tuene/Ostrowksi project (Jacob, Ostrowski, and Teune: 1993; Jacob, Linder, Nabholz and Heirli: 1999) – or in European groupings. Again the work of Kjellberg is important in this context (*International Political Science Review*: 1980; Dente and Kjellberg: 1986; Hoffman-Martinot and Kjellberg: 1996), along with that of Sharpe (1979); Norton (1994); this author in association with Page (Page and Goldsmith:1987) and Wolman (Wolman and Goldsmith: 1992)[16], as well as that of Hesse and Sharpe (1991), together with the consistently stimulating contributions of Keating (1991; 1995 and

---

15 See for example the work of Harding (1995; 1997; 2000); LeGalès (2003); John and Cole (2001)
16 See Page and Goldsmith (1987); Page 1992; Goldsmith and Wolman (1992); Goldsmith (1995); Goldsmith (1996).

22

1998), Loughlin (2001), Cauflield and Larsen (2002) and John (2001). At the same time, one would highlight the work of Scandinavians such as Baldersheim and Stahlberg (1994; 1999); Germans such as Wollman (2000b); Kersting and Vetter (2003); Gabriel (2000); Vetter (2002); French scholars such as LeGalès (2003); Balme et al. (1999), Hoffman-Martinot (1996; 2000); Dutch scholars such as Denters (2005) and Toonen (1991) or the work by US scholars such as Sellers (2002). The result of all this work is that there is now a substantial body of knowledge that attempts to relate emerging developments in local/regional government within particular countries to developments in a larger, mainly European context, with the beginnings of theoretical frameworks designed to consider such developments emerging.

Having said that, it is probably true to say that empirical theory remains a weakness at the European level in the field, notwithstanding the importance of the work of people like Rhodes (1997) on policy networks or Harding on urban theory (2005) or Wollman (2000a; 2000b) with the use of path dependency models.

The New Research Agenda

Again as with the review of past developments, consideration of the future research agenda must inevitably reflect individual prejudices. Others will no doubt provide their own lists. I also would not wish my agenda to indicate any sense of priority – except perhaps in relation to one item. That item concerns the growing amount of work that indicates the increasing divergence which has emerged and continues to do so both *between* regions/ cities/localities around the world and *within* them. If the gap between rich and poor continues to widen, both within and between territories, then the potential for conflict is likely to be increased – yet the potential for *any individual* territory to solve its problems is increasingly minimal in the face of continuing globalization. In this context, most recently (and in so far as time permits) I have found myself turning to the International Relations literature to see whether it offers useful insights (especially on the European Union), and I would suggest that useful dialogues between the two academic communities might be of interest in studying some issues on the urban politics/local government agenda[17]. But generally more work on the causes, consequences and possible solutions of the growing divergence between and within regions/cities and localities would be desirable.

In this context, I am conscious of how *Western European/British/ developed world* this contribution has been. But, again as data reveal, the real

---

17 See for example the special issue of *Etudes Internationales* edited by Jacques Palard on the international relaitons of European regions (Etudes Internationales, 1999. vol 30 no 4.

growth in urban politics/local government is in the third rather than the developed world. It is to the latter to which I believe more attention should be paid, given the rate of urbanization in countries like China, continents like Asia generally, and in Latin America. The speed of change in these countries/areas is so much faster than anything Europe or indeed North America has known – yet we know relatively little about processes of urban politics and local government in these countries. The world's largest cities are not in the United States or Europe, but in India, Brazil and Mexico or China. We need to know more about urban politics in these countries[18]

I allow myself one final third priority, that of theory, both normative and empirical. We need more and better explanations, ones which reflect the present day experience of the 21st century and not that of the 19th or indeed which hark back to the heyday of recent social/political science developments of the sixties and early seventies. The nineties – at least in Britain – did see a return to a concern with the exercise of power in cities (Dowding et al.: 2000; Harding: 2000), perhaps without adding much to the debate. Writing in 1998 Stoker drew attention to what he called contextual theory and regulation theory – neo/post Marxist/critical approaches to the study of urban politics (Jessop: 1996; 2000; Painter: 1995; 2000) – which can be contrasted with neo-liberal rational choice approaches such as those adopted by Dunleavy and his associates. (Dowding et al.: 2000). Wollman (1999) (2000a; 2000b) drew attention to the importance of path dependency approaches (the impact of past history and culture on present day politics and policies) to the understanding of urban politics. What all these approaches suggest is that 'what is characteristic of urban political science in contrast to some other areas of the discipline is its openness to new theoretical and methodological approaches and its willingness to be cross-fertilized by insights from other disciplines' (Stoker: 1998: 127). This characteristic of a diversity of approach and openness to new ideas is a particular strength of the field, one that we should value in future.

Those who have concerned themselves with the study of local government and urban politics have long been accused of being involved with the 'Cinderella' of the discipline (Banfield: 1975), dealing with an area seen as unimportant within the political science profession. One would hope this review and its associated future agenda would suggest that, far from being unimportant, the field could well be at the discipline's centre: what other field offers so many difficult questions to research, and yet also offers such fertile ground for comparative work of an innovative nature and the possibilities of new theoretical insights. Long may it continue to do so!

---

18 See for example some of the contributions in Watson and Gibson (1998); on Bombay see Patel (1998) and Mehta (2004); on Thailand see Shalker (2004);on Mexico City see Cross (1998), and on Sao Paulo see Marques and Bichir (2004). More generally see Amen (2006 in print).

References

Almond, G./Verba, S. (1963): *The Civic Culture*, Princeton, N.J.: Princeton University Press.

Amen, M. (2006 in print): *Relocating Global Cities from the Center to the Margin*, Oxford: Rowman and Littlefield.

Andrew, C./Goldsmith, M. (eds.) (1998): *New Trends in Municipal Government*, IPSR vol 18 no 2.

Baldersheim, H./Balme, R./Clark, T.N./Hoffmann-Martinot, V./Magnusson, H. (eds.) (1989): *New Leaders, Parties and Groups: Comparative Tendencies in Local leadership*, Paris: CERVEL.

Baldersheim, H./Illner, M./Offerdahl, A./Rose, L./Swianniewicz, P. (1996): *Local Democracy and the Processes of Transformation in East-Central Europe*, Boulder: Westview.

Baldersheim, H./Stahlberg, K. (1994): *Towards the Self-Regulating Municipality*. Free communes and modernization in Scandinavia, Aldershot: Ashgate.

Baldersheim, H./Stahlberg, K. (eds.) (1999): *Nordic Region Building in a European Perspective*, Aldershot: Ashgate.

Balme, R. (ed.) (1996): *Les Politiques du neo-regionalisme*, Paris: Economica

Balme, R./Faure, A./Mabileau, A. (eds.) (1999): *Les Nouvelles Politiques Locales*, Paris: Presses de Sciences Po.

Banfield, E.C./Wilson, J. (1963): *City Politics*, Cambridge, Mass: Harvard University Press.

Banfield, E.C. (1975): 'Foreword' in: Young, K. (ed.): *Essays in the Study of Urban Politics*, London: Macmillan, pp.vi-xi.

Boaden, N. (1971): *Urban Policy Making*, Cambridge: CUP.

Boyne, G. (1985): 'Review Article; Theory, methodology and results in Political Science – The case of output studies', *British Journal of Political Science*, vol 15 pp. 473-515.

Bulpitt, J. (1967): *Party Politics in English Local Government*, London: Longman.

Bulpitt, J. (1983): *Territory and Power in the United Kingdom*, Manchester: Manchester University Press.

Castells, M. (1975): *The Urban Question*, London: Edward Arnold.

Castells, M. (1979): *City, Class and Power*, London: Macmillan.

Caulfield, E./Larsen, H. (eds.) (2002): *Local government at the Millenium*, Opladen: Leske + Budrich.

Clark, T./Hoffmann-Martinot, V. (eds.) (1998): *The New Political Culture*, Boulder: Westview.

Clark, T./Ferguson, L. (1983): *City Money*, Urbana, Ill: University of Illinois and University of Chicago.

Cochrane, A. (1993): *Whatever Happened to Local Government?* Buckingham: Open University Press.

Cross, J. (1998): *Informal Politics. Street Vendors and the State in Mexico City*, Stanford: Stanford University Press.

Crozier, M. (1976): *The Bureaucratic Phenomenon*, Chicago: Chicago University Press.

Crozier, M./Thoenig, J. (1976): 'The Regulation of Complex Organised Systems', *Administrative Science Quarterly*, vol 21 pp 547-570.

Dahl, R. A. (1961): *Who Governs?* New Haven: Yale University Press.

Danielson, M.N. (1971) (ed.): *Metroppolitan Politics: A Reader*, 2nd Edition, Boston: Little Brown.

Danziger, J. (1979): *Making Budgets*, London: Sage

Davies, B. (1968): *Social Needs and Resources in Local Services*, London: Michael Joseph.

Davies, B. (1975): In: Young, K. (ed.) *Essays in the Study of Urban Politics*, London: Macmillan.

Dearlove, J. (1979): *The Reorganisation of British Local Government*, Cambridge: CUP.

Dearlove, J. (1973): *The Politics of Policy in Local Government*, Cambridge: CUP.

Dente, B./Kjellberg, F. (1988): *The Dynamics of Institutional Change*, London: Sage.

Denters, B./Rose, L. (eds.) (2005): *Comparing Local Governance: Trends and Developments.*, Basingstoke: Palgrave. (in press).

Dowding, K./Dunleavy, P./King, D./Margetts, H./Rydin, Y. (2000): 'Understanding Urban Governance: the contribution of Rational choice' in: Stoker, G. (ed.): *The New Politics of British Local Governance*, London: Macmillan, pp. 91-116.

Dunleavy, P. (1980): *Urban Political Analysis*, London: Macmillan.

Dye, T. (1966): *Politics, Economics and the Public Policy Outcomes in American States*, Chicago: Rand Mcnally.

Fainstein, S./Fainstein, N./Hill, R.C./Judd, D./Smith, M.P. (1986): *Restructuring the City*, New York: Longman.

Fraser, D. (1976): *Urban Politics in Victorian England*, Leicester: Leicester University Press.

Gabriel, O./Hoffman-Martinot, V./Savitch, H. (eds.) (2000): *Urban Democracy*, Opladen: Leske + Budrich.

Goldsmith, M. (1995): 'Autonomy and City Limits'. In: Judge/Stoker/Wollmann (eds.): *Theories of Urban Politics*, London: Sage, pp. 228-252.

Goldsmith, M. (1996): 'Normative Theories of Local Government – a European comparison'. In: King, D./Stoker, G. (eds.): *Rethinking Local Democracy*, London: Macmillan pp. 174-192.

Goldsmith, M. (2004): 'Central control over Local Government: A West European Comparison'. In: Carmichael, P./Midwinter, A. (eds.): *Regulating Local Authorities*, London: Cass pp. 91-112.

Goldsmith, M. (2005): 'A New Intergovernmentalism?' in: Denters, B./Rose, L. (eds.): *Comparing Local Governance*, Basingstoke: Palgrave.

Goldsmith, M./Klaussen, K.K. (eds.) (1997): *European Iintegration and Local Government*, Cheltenham: Edward Elgar.

Goldsmith, M./Villadsen, S. (eds.) (1986): *Urban Political Theory and the Management of Fiscal Stress*, Aldershot: Gower.

Green, D. (1967): *Community Decision Making in a Georgian City*, unpublished PhD, University of Bath.

Gremion. P. (1976): *Le Pouvoir Peripherique*, Le Seuil: Paris

Gunlicks, A.B. (1981): *Local Government Reform and Reorganization*, London: Kennikat.

Gurr, T./King, D. (1987): *State and the City*, Chicago: University of Chicago Press.

Gustafsson, G. (1981): 'Local Government Reform in Sweden' in: Gunlicks, A. (ed.): *Local Government Reform and Reorganization*, Port Washington: Kennikat.

Habermas, J. (1976): *Legitimation Crisis*, London: Heinemann.

Hampton, W. (1970): *Democracy and Community*, Oxford: OUP.

Hanf, K. and Scharpf, F. (1978) (eds.): *Interorganizational Policy Making*, London: Sage.

Harding, A. (1995): 'Elite Theory and Growth Machines'. In: Judge, D./Stoker, G./ Wolman, H. (eds.): *Theories of Urban Politics*, London: Sage pp. 35-53.

Harding, A. (2000): 'Regime Formation in Manchester and Edinburgh'. In: Stoker, G. (ed.) *The New Politics of British Local Governance*, London: Macmillan, pp. 54-71.

Harding, A. (2005): *Urban Political Theory*, London: Routledge (forthcoming)

Harding, A./LeGalès, P. (1997): 'Globalization, Urban Policy and Urban Change'. In: Scott, A. (ed.): *The Limits of Globalization,* London: Routledge.

Harvey, D. (1973): *Social Justice and the City*, London: Edward Arnold.

Heinelt, H./Kubler, D. (2005): *Metropolitan Government and Governance*, London: Routledge.

Hendricks, F./Tops, P. (1999): 'Between Democracy and Efficiency: Trends in Local Government Reform in the Netherlands and Germany' *Public Administration*, vol 77 no 1 pp133-153.

Hennock, E.P. (1973): *Fit and Proper Persons*, London: Edward Arnold.

Hesse, J.J./Sharpe, L.J. (eds.) (1991): *Local government and Urban Affairs in International Perspective*, Baden-Baden: Nomos Verlagsgesellschaft.

Hofferbert, R.I. (1975): *The Study of Public Policy*, New York: Bobbs Merrill

Hoffman-Martinot, V. (2000): 'The Fragmented Democracy of Big Cities'. In: Gabriel, O./Hoffman-Martinot, V./Savitch, H. (eds.): *Urban Democracy*, Opladen: Leske + Budrich.

Hoffman-Martinot, V./Kjellberg, F. (eds.) (1996): *Decentraliser en France et en Norvege*, Paris: Pedone.

Hoffman-Martinot, V./Rallings, C./Thrasher (1996): 'Comparing Local Electoral Turnout in Britain and France, *European Journal of Political Research*, vol 30 no 4.

Hooghe, L. (ed.) (1996): *Cohesion Policy and European Integration*, Oxford: Clarendon Press.

Hooghe, L./Marks, G. (2001): *Multi-Level Governance and European Integration*, Oxford: Rowman and Littlefield.

Hunter, F. (1953): *Community Power Structure*, Chapel Hill: University of North Carolina Press.

Jacob, B./Ostrowki, K./Teune, H. (eds.) (1993): *Democracy and Local Governance*, Hawaii: University of Hawaii Press.

Jacob, B./Linder, W./Nabholz, R./Heirli, C. (eds.) (1999): *Democracy and Local Governance*, Bern: University of Bern.

Jeffery, C. (ed.) (1997): *Regions and the EU*, London: Frank Cass.

Jessop, B. (1996): 'A Neo-Gramscian Approach to the Regulation of Urban Regimes: Accumulation Strategies, Hegemonic Projects and Governance'. In: Lasuria, M. (ed.): *Reconstructing Urban Regime Theory*, London: Sage.

Jessop, B. (2000): 'Governance Failure'. In: Stoker, G. (ed.): *The New Politics of British Local Governance*, London: Macmillan, pp. 11-32.

John, P. (2001): *Local governance in Western Europe*, London: Sage.

John, P./Cole, A. (2000): *Local Governance in England and France*, London: Routledge.

Jones, B./Keating, M. (eds.) (1995): *The European Union and the Regions*, Oxford: Clarendon Press.

Jones, G. (1969): *Borough Politics*, London: Macmillan.

Jouve, B./Lefevre, C. (eds.) (1999): *Villes, Metropoles*, Paris: Anthropos.

Judge, D./Stoker, G./Wolman, H. (eds.) (1996): *Theories of Urban Politics*, London: Sage.

Kaplan, H. (1982): *Reform, Planning and City Politics: Montreal, Winnipeg, Toronto, Toronto*: Univ of Toronto Press.

Katznelson, I. (1992): *Marxism and the City*, Oxford: Oxford University Press.

Keating, M. (1991): *Comparative Urban Politics*, Aldershot: Edward Elgar.

Keating, M./Loughlin, J. (eds.) (1997): *The Political Economy of Regionalism*, London: Frank Cass.

Keating, M. (1998): *The New Regionalism in Western Europe*, Aldershot: Edward Elgar.

Kersting, N./Vetter, A. (eds.) (2003): *Reforming Local Government in Europe*, Opladen: Leske + Budrich.

King, D./Pierre, J. (eds.) (1990): *Challenges to Local Government*, London: Sage.

Klaussen, K.K./Stahlberg, K. (1998): *New Public Management in Norden*, Odebse: Odense University Press.

Lane, J. (1997): 'Public Sector Reform in the Nordic Countries'. In: Lane, J.-E. (ed.) *Public Sector Reform*, London: Sage.

Lee, J. M. (1963): *Social Leaders and Public Persons*, Oxford: OUP.

Leemans, A.F. (1972): 'The Dutch decentralization system in transition', *Planning and Development in the Netherlands* vol 6 no 2 pp. 93-107.

Lefevre, C. (1998): 'Meropolitan Government and Governance in Western Countries: A Critical Review', *International Journal of Urban and Regional Research*, vol 22 pp. 2-25.

LeGalès, P. (1995): 'Du gouvernement local a la gouvernance urbaine' *Revue Francaise de Sciences Politiques*, vol 45.

LeGalès, P. (1998): 'Regulations and governance in European cities', *International Journal of Urban and Regional Research*, vol 22, pp. 482-506.

LeGalès, P. (2003): *European Cities*, Cambridge: CUP.

LeGalès, P./Lequesne, C. (eds.) (1997): *Regions in Europe*, London; Routledge.

Leresche, J.-P./Joye, D./Bassand, D. (eds.) (1995): *Metropolitisations*, Geneva: George.

Lojkin, J. (1976): 'Contribution to a Marxist theory of capitalist urbanisation'. In: Pickvance, C. (ed.): *Urban Sociology; Critical Essays*, London: Tavistock.

Loughlin, J. (1996): 'Representing the Regions in Europe: The Committee of the Regions' *Regional and Federal Studies* vol 6 no 2 pp. 147-165.

Loughlin, J. (2001): *Sub-National Government in the European Union*, Oxford: Oxford.

Marks, G./Scharpf, F./Schmitter, P.C./Streeck, W. (1996): *Governance in the European Union*, London: Sage.

Marques, E.C./Bichir, R.M. (2003): 'Public policies, politicaa cleavage and urban space: state infrastructure policies in Sao Paulo', *International Journal of Urban and Regional Research*, vol 27 no 4 pp. 811-827.

Mehta, S. (2004): *Bombay Lost and Found*, New York: Alfred Knopf.

Mollenkopf, J. (1983): *The Contested City*, Princeton: Princeton University Press.

Mollenkopf, J./Castells, M. (eds.) (1991): *Dual City*, New York: Russell Sage Foundation.

Morlan, R. (1981): 'Local Government Reorganization in the Netherlands'. In: Gunlicks, A. (ed.): *Local Government Reform and Reorganization*, Port Washington; Kennikat, pp. 42-53.

Mouritzen, P.- E. (1991): *Den Politiske Cyclus*, Aarhus: Forlaget Politica.

Mouritzen, P.-E. (ed.) (1992): *Managing Cities in Austerity*, London: Sage.

Newton, K. (1976): *Second City Politics*, Oxford; OUP.

Newton, K. (1980): *Balancing the Books*, London: Sage.

Newton, K. (1969): 'City Politics in Britain and the United States', *Political Studies*, vol 17 no 2, pp. 208-218.

Newton, K. (1976): *Second City Politics*, Oxford: OUP.

Newton, K./Sharpe, L.J. (1977): 'Local Outputs Research: some reflections and proposals', *Policy and Politics*, vol 5 no 3 pp. 61-82.

Nicholson, R./Topham, N. (1971): 'The determinants of investment in housing by local authorities', *Journal of the Royal Statistical Society,* series A, vol 134, no 3 pp. 273-303.

Norton, A. (1994): *International Handbook on Local and Regional Government*, Cheltenham: Edward Elgar.

Offe, C. (1976): *Industry and Inequality*, London: Edward Arnold.

Offe, C. (1984): *Contradictions of the Welfare State*, London: Hutchinson.

Osborne, D./Gaebler, T. (1993): *Reinventing Government*, Reading, Mass: Addison-Wesley.

Page, E. (1991): *Localism and Centralism*, Oxford: OUP.

Page, E./Goldsmith, M. (1987): *Central-Local Relations in Unitary States*, London: Sage

Pahl, R. (1975): *Whose City?* London: 1975.

Painter, J. (1995): 'Regulation Theory, Post-Fordism and Urban Politics'. In: Judge, D./Stoker, G./Wolman, H. (eds.): *Theories of Urban Politics*, London: Sage, pp. 276-296.

Painter, J./Goodwin, M, (2000): 'Local government after Fordism'. In: Stoker, G. (ed.): *The New Politics of British Local Governance*, London: Macmillan, pp. 33-53.

Palard, J. (1999): 'The International Relations of European Cities', Special issue of *Etudes Internationales*, vol 30 no 4.

Parkinson, M. (1986): *Liverpool on the Brink*, London: Policy Journals.

Patel, S. (1998): *Bombay*, Oxford India: Oxford University Press.

Pettersen, P.-A./Rose, L.E. (1999): 'Participation in Local Politics in Norway: Some Do, Some Don't; Some Will, Some Won't' *Political Behavior*, vol 18 no 1, pp51-98.

Pickvance, C. (1976) (ed.): *Urban Sociology: Critical Essays*, London: 1975.

Pickvance, C. (1996): 'Marxist Theories of Urban Politics' in: Judge, D./Stoker, G./ Wolman, H. (eds.): *Theories of Urban Politics*, London: Sage, pp. 253-275.

Preteceille, E./Pickvance, C. (1991): *State Restructuring and Local Power*, London: Pinter.

Putnam, R. (1993): *Making Democracy Work: Civil Traditions in Modern Italy*, Princeton, Nj: Princeton University Press.

Putnam, R. (2000): *Bowling Alone*, New York: Simon and Schuster.

Rhodes, G. (1970): *The Government of London: the struggle for reform*, London: Allen and Unwin.

Rhodes, R. (1981): *Control and Power in Central-Local government Relations*, Aldershot: Gower.

Rhodes, R. (1986): *National World of Local Government*, London: Allen and Unwin.

Rhodes, R. (1988): *Beyond Westminster and Whitehall*, London: Unwin Hyman.

Rhodes, R. (1997): Understanding Governance: Policy Networks, Reflexivity and Accountability, Buckingham: Open University Press.

Rose, L.E./Pettersen, P.-A. (1999): 'Confidence in Politicians and Institutions: Comparing National and Local Levels'. In: Narud, H.N./Aalberg, T. (eds.): *Challenges to Representative Democracy: Parties, Voters and Public Opinion*, Bergen: Fagbokforlaget.

Rose, L.E./Pettersen, P.-A. (2000): 'The Legitimacy of Local Government: What Makes a Difference? Evidence from Norway'. In: Hoggart, K./Clark, T.N. (eds.): *Citizen Responsive Government*, Amsterdam: JAI/Elsevier. Research in Urban Policy, vol 8.

Rose, R. (1983): *Understanding the UK*, London: Longman.

Sassen, S. (1991): *The Global City: London, New York, Tokyo*, Princeton, NJ: Princeton University Press.

Sassen, S. (2004): *Cities in the World Economy*, Thousand Oaks: Pine Forge Press.

Saunders, P. (1975): 'They make the Rules', *Policy and Politics*, vol. 4, pp. 31-58.

Saunders, P. (1979): *Urban Politics – a sociological analysis*, London: Hutchinson.

Saunders, P. (1986): 'Reflections on the dual state thesis: the argument, its origins and its critics.' In: Goldsmith, M./Villadsen, S. (eds): *Urban Political Theory and the Management of Fiscal Stress*, Aldershot: Gower pp 1-40.

Savitch, H./Vogel, R. (1996): *Regional Politics*, London: Sage.

Schattsneider, E.E. (1960): *The Semi-Sovereign People*, New York: Holt, Rinehart and Winston.

Sellers, J. (2002): *Governing from Below*, Cambridge: CUP.

Shalkin, G. (2004): 'Globalization and local leadership: Growth, Power and Politics in Thailand's Eastern Seaboard', *International Journal of Urban and Regional Research*, vol 28 no 1 pp. 11-26.

Sharkansky, I. (1970): *Policy Analysis in Political Science*, Chicago: Markham.

Sharpe, L.J. (ed.) (1967): *Voting in Cities*, London: Macmillan.

Sharpe, L.J. (1981): *The Local Fiscal Crisis in Western Europe*, London: Sage.

Sharpe, L.J./Newton, K. (1984): *Does Politics Matter*, Oxford: OUP.

Sharpe, L.J. (ed.) (1979): *Decentralist Trends in Western Democracies*, London: Sage.

Sharpe, L.J. (ed.): (1983): *The Rise of Meso Government in Europe*, London: Sage.

Smallwood, F. (1965): *Greater London: the politics of metropolitan reform*, New York: Bobbs Merrill.

Smith, M.P. (1988): *City, State and Market*, Oxford: Blackwells.

Stanyer, J. (1975) in Young K (ed): *Essays in the Study of Urban Politics*, London: Macmillan.

Stoker, G. (1991): *The Politics of Local Government* (2nd Edition), London: Macmillan.

Stoker, G. (1998): 'Theory and Urban Politics', IPSR vol 18 no 2 pp. 119-131.

Stoker, G. (ed.) (2000): *The New Politics of British Local Governance*, London: Macmillan.

Stoker, G. (2004): *Transforming Local Governance*, Basingstoke: Palgrave.

Stoker, G./King, D. (eds.) (1996): *Understanding Local Democracy*, Basingstoke: MacMillan.

Stone, C. (1989): *Regime Politics: Governing Atlanta, 1946-1988*, Lawrence: Kansas University Press.

Toonen, T. (1991): 'Change in Continuity: Local Governemnt and Urban Affairs in the Netherlands' in: Hesse, J.J./Sharpe, L.J. (eds.): *Local Government and Urban Affairs in International Perspective*, Baden-Baden: Nomos Verlagsgesellschaft.

Vetter, A. (2002): *Lokale Politic als Ressource der Demokratie in Europa?* Opladen: Leske + Budrich.

Villadsen, S. (1986): 'The dual state and corpotatism: reflections in the light of Danish experience'. In: Goldsmith, M./Villadsen, S. (eds.): *Urban Political Theory and the Management of Fiscal Stress*, Aldershot: Gower, pp. 41-62.

Watson, S./Gibson, K. (1998): *Postmodern Cities and Spaces*, Oxford: Blackwell.

Wilson, D./Game, C. (2002): *Local Government in the United Kindom*, Basingstoke: Palgrave.

Wollmann, H./Goldsmith, M. (1992): *Urban Politics and Policy*, Oxford: Blackwell.

Wollmann, H. (2000a): 'Local Government Modernization in Germany: Between Incrementalism and Reform Waves', *Public Administration*, vol 28 no 4, pp. 291-332.

Wollmann, H. (2000b): 'Local Government Structures: from historic divergence towards convergence', *Government and Policy*, vol 18, no 1 pp. 33-56.

Wollmann H./Roth R. (eds.) (1999): *Kommunalpolitik*, Opladen: Leske + Budrich.

Wood, B. (1976): *The Process of Local Government Reform*, 1977-74, London: Allen and Unwin.

Young, K. (1975): *Essays in the Study of Urban Politics*, Basingstoke: Macmillan.

Chapter 2
Globalisation and the Study of Local Politics: Is the Study of Local Politics Meaningful in a Global Age?

Susan E. Clarke

I. Normative, theoretical, and empirical dimensions

Thinking about the study of local politics in a global era raises normative, theoretical, and empirical issues[1]. Normatively, a classic argument contends that the vitality of broader democratic practices is contingent on the vitality of local democracy (Gabriel et al. 2000; Held 1999). In the absence of local democracy or under conditions of weak local democracy, the prospects for democracy at national levels are problematic (Vetter 2000). Rather than see local politics as a separate sphere, whose significance rises and falls in response to external trends, many theorists point out that local politics are critical arenas for learning the civic skills necessary for democratic practice. For many citizens, the most critical issues demanding political responses are everyday concerns that are the responsibility of local officials. From this perspective, the study of local politics is necessary and inherently meaningful independent of the larger context.

Questioning the contemporary significance of studying local politics often implies a series of assumptions about how changes in this larger context might alter the role of local governments (Hambleton et al. 2002; McNeill 1999). In particular the technological, spatial, and social changes attendant to globalization initially seemed to call these local roles into question. They not only appeared to challenge the salience of local politics in a period of global transformation and reterritorialization, they opened the door to new forms of democratic practice – particularly through use of new information technologies – that could potentially displace the very face-to-face political engagement that makes local politics so necessary to democratic vitality. Many of these trends also appeared to threaten any notion of local autonomy and discretion; local governments may remain viable units but the policy options available to them in the face of global competitive pressures can be circumscribed and thin.

These normative issues encourage a more systematic assessment of the links between local politics and globalization. Rather than see the significance of local politics as driven – and perhaps diminished – by globalization,

---

1   I appreciate the research assistance provided by Luis Torres and Cindy Cooley in collecting the diverse materials considered here.

most scholars now focus on the ways in which the global and the local are mutually constitutive. That is, globalization is shaped and articulated through state institutional frameworks and governance processes at multiple scales, including the local. As these processes unfold, the configuration of state power at different scales is restructured as well.

Two research literatures are available to guide our examination of global-local links and the continued significance of local politics. One consists of theoretical frameworks explicitly theorizing global-local links: this includes the world cities framework and a cluster of theories centered on reterritorialization or rescaling processes.[2] A second literature includes reconceptualizations of more familiar approaches to local politics to take into account the impacts of globalization. These approaches include urban regime analysis, governance arrangements, cultural approaches, and policy agenda studies. In both sets of literatures, there is a consistent concern with the effects of globalization on local inequalities and social cohesion. More specific analyses of local politics put additional emphasis on how the economic, spatial, social, and cultural impacts of globalization affect the distribution of power within localities.

This essay sketches the contours of these literatures, highlighting the findings generated by these approaches that help us address our basic question – the continuing salience of local politics in a global era. It then considers the dark side of globalization – terrorism – and its impacts on local politics. Finally, the link between community and democracy is revisited in terms of the prospects for democratic inclusion. This overview indicates that localities and local politics are key venues for globalization and state restructuring processes but that traditional political science concepts and approaches may not be sufficient for analysis of local politics in a global age.

II. Theorizing Global-Local Links

One of the initial interpretations of globalization processes suggested "the death of distance" – an argument that increased capital mobility and new information technologies made place or location irrelevant (Cairncross 2001). If not irrelevant, at least interchangeable: with the declining significance of proximity for many economic processes, any number of locations was suitable for capital investment. Variations in the traditional factor of

---

2   Brenner defines "rescaling" as "the production, reconfiguration or contestation of particular differentiations, orderings and hierarchies among geographical scales" (Brenner 2001: 600). This focus on scale and rescaling asserts that space is a critical aspect of the workings of capitalism and emphasizes the importance of urban and regional sites – or scales – for political transformations attendant to globalization (See Brenner 2004).

34

production costs – land, labor, capital – that influenced the desirability and prosperity of individual cities now appeared to be smoothed out by these new technologies. With many cities equally attractive investment sites, the distinctive features of any city were less salient. From this perspective, investment interests enjoyed a global menu of possible locations; the specific locale, and seemingly even the national setting, appeared immaterial. The competitive pressures on all cities increased and, as a result, the possibilities of local discretion appeared to shrink. Under these conditions, local politics indeed appeared to be insignificant.

These initial perspectives enjoyed more political appeal, especially in the United States and Great Britain, than scholarly staying power. As scholars began empirical assessments of the impacts of globalization it became clear that these were uneven and incomplete processes; they became layered on to other processes shaping local politics rather than becoming determinant factors. Nor were they mechanical, universalistic, or automatic forces; their impacts were often contested and challenged, often at the subnational rather than the national level. Although some factor costs were homogenized by globalization and economic restructuring processes, other locational features became more important as new economic sectors began to drive growth. In short, locations remained salient although ranked now by new criteria.

Paradoxically, local politics can also be seen as becoming more important with the advent of globalization. This stems from the need to "ground" or "pin down" capital and economic activities in particular locales; local political choices could influence which locales were most conducive to doing so. The success of national economies in global competition appears tied to encouraging more entrepreneurial and competitive local governments. Locales also serve as sites in a transnational network of organizations meeting to conduct "the work of globalization" such as the G7, the WTO, and the World Bank as well as of anti-globalization organizations linked in their protest of these efforts (Martinotti and Pozzi 2004).

A. The World City Framework

In embracing this seemingly paradoxical view of the increasing importance of the local in a global era, the world city perspective emphasizes the emergence of a new global hierarchy of cities. The concept of a "world city" or "global city" emerged in the mid-1980s (Sassen 1984; Friedman 1986; also, see Knox and Taylor 1995; Abu-Lughod 1999; White 1998; Bliss 2004) to direct attention to the changing roles of major cities in a global economy. The conceptualizations varied somewhat: Friedman (1986, 318) presented the world city hypothesis as "the form and extent of a city's integration with the world economy and the functions assigned to the city in the new spatial division of labour will be decisive for any structural changes occurring within it." To Sassen (1991), the emergence of this global division of labor prompted the rise of global cities as the sites of the agglomeration of advanced producer services – the key economic command and control functions in a global economy. As strategic nodes in a new economy of globalized commerce, financial, telecommunication, and information flows, cities such as London, New York, and Tokyo form a top tier in a new global urban hierarchy. They also became spaces of stark polarization, bringing together great wealth and great poverty as poorly-paid service workers supported the functioning of finance, producer services, and information sectors.

The world city concept engenders categorizations of cities in terms of these agglomerations, resulting in a hierarchy crowned by a few world cities most intensely involved in core command functions. Whatever the hierarchical rank, the assumption was that city economies increasingly are structured by the same global market rationality and division of labor; a city's rank in the global hierarchy, determined by the functional role it plays in the globalization process and its share of these command functions, determines its fate (Hill 2004). Over time, the assumption is that cities have more in common with other cities at similar "ranks" than with cities within their own national boundaries.

Many critiques of this argument emerged from efforts to subject the global city hypothesis to empirical testing. On the ground, it appears that the effects of globalization on the economic context of large cities are more context-specific and more nuanced than the broad theory anticipates. Indeed, some critiques question the seemingly universalistic sweep of the argument (Hill and Kim 2000). Some world city scholars now argue that regionality is at least as important as hierarchy among world cities (Taylor 2004). These regional patternings indicate that globalization is not the homogenizing, universalistic process sometimes depicted; rather the engagement of the global and the local is shaped by many factors, including state forces. To Hill (2004: 374; Hill and Fujita 2003), these patternings resemble nested hierarchies: along with increasing interdependence, there is differentiation within and among regional, national, and city levels so that cities' economic base, spatial organization, and social structure are shaped at multiple levels and therefore differ.

Knowing a city's rank in the global hierarchy, therefore, is not sufficient; it is necessary to understand the nested configuration in which they function (Hill 2004: 376). This includes, according to Janet Abu-Lughod (1999), cities' history and their institutional political structures; these features ensure that globalization processes produce different economic, spatial, and social effects in cities. They also raise the prospect that city responses to globalization may be path dependent (see also Hill 2004), structured by local institutional configurations and the heavy hand of history. This contextual perspective also directs attention to the ways in which cities are embedded in multi-

36

level governance structures. Whether we analyze cities in the context of nested hierarchies (Hill 2004), in terms of multi-level institutional infrastructures (Sellers 2002), or as actors in more or less integrated intergovernmental structures (Savitch and Kantor 2001), a more relational view of local agency underscores both the opportunities and constraints created by these external structures. As Hill argues, "a city can only achieve and sustain world city status with the political, administrative, and ideological assistance of a powerful state" (Hill 2004: 378).

This emphasis on differentiation and contingency also emerges from critiques of the world city hypothesis focused on its political implications (Evans 1997; Smith 2001). In contrast to the structuralist orientation of the original conceptualizations, scholars emphasize the role of political agency in creating distinctive global-local links on a city by city and region by region basis. Sassen and others do not ignore agency; indeed many see global cities competing for the transnational financial and corporate elites in growth sectors as a deliberate economic development strategy. But the emphasis on internal assets as shaping a city's competitiveness is countered by arguments that it is the inter-connectivity and cooperation among cities, firms, the state, and sectoral interests that both shapes a global network of cities and determines a city's place within in it (Beaverstock et al. 1999) Rather than a static hierarchy reflecting city functions, a global network of cities is created and sustained by the cooperative as well as competitive efforts of sets of actors rooted in particular geographic settings (Beaverstock et al. 2002).

Evans (2002), Smith (2001), and others point to a range of non-elite political actors also engaged in negotiating these global-local links, including transnational anti-globalization, human rights, and environmental groups. Indeed, Smith argues that many cities socially construct elements of world city-ness through such networks, leading him to argue for a "transnational urbanism" rather than a hierarchy of world cities. These ties also are the grounds for challenges to globalization, such as "the battle in Seattle" and other venues attracting demonstrations against international organizations such as the WTO (Levi and Olson 2000; Martinotti and Pozzi 2004). As this suggests, social movements no longer necessarily target national states and even 'urban' social movements are no longer limited by locale. Rather Guidry et al. (2000) argue that globalization supports the formation of issue-based "transnational public spheres" in which global-local alliances may transform identities as the basis for collective action. Increasingly, these are local actions challenging globalization processes; the economic impacts of globalization on cities create greater inequalities but also open new prospects for activism (Hamel et al. 2000).

B. Cities, Regions, and Nation States

Another emerging paradigm makes sense of these global-local linkages by emphasizing their spatial dimensions – the rescaling of urban governance. This is a looser cluster of approaches rather than a coherent theoretical statement as in the world cities hypothesis. They contrast with the initial deterritorialization logic of globalization – that globalization meant the declining importance of territory, including the decline of the nation state. Rather, the core argument anticipates a process of reterritorialization of state institutions and rescaling of political relations attendant to globalization of economic activities and restructuring of state processes (Brenner 2002: 4; Scott et al. 2001). The focus on reterritorialization and rescaling processes underscores the spatial dimension of globalization. It rejects the contention that globalization is "flattening" space into a homogenous plane and emphasizes the significance of emerging and restructuring institutions in a variety of territorial spaces or arenas. Local politics, therefore, occurs in a context of ongoing and simultaneous processes of economic globalization and localization. The key research issue in these arguments is the relations between scales and their impact on local politics. Rather than seeing these scales as "geological layers" (Beauregard 1995), the focus is on "the politics of scale" (Brenner 2002, 2004; Delaney and Leitner 1997) – how they are constituted through negotiations and conflicts among institutions across scales. This emphasis on intentionality and constructivism leads us to anticipate and analyze continuing struggles and negotiations over global-local links at different scales (Clarke 2002; Smith 1998).

Some of these arguments can be traced back to the world city debates. The sense that some cities operate in a borderless space, largely independent of the nation state in which they are embedded, is one of the implications of the initial world city arguments. Does the emergence of global cities necessarily mean a decline in importance and power of the nation state? Or as some scholars see it, do world cities "need" the larger state? A zero-sum assumption of the relative power of national and local entities is misleading. At a minimum, globalization destabilizes these scalar relations and historical patterns. Initial characterizations of the "hollowing out" of the state system – authority and influence is moving up to supranational entities, down to subnational levels, and out to nongovernmental organizations – are now amplified by considering the counter-trends to these state restructuring processes (Jessop 1999; Brenner 2003). These counter-trends involve active efforts by national governments to regulate these new sites of state power created through apparent hollowing out processes (Brenner 2003, 2004).

In contrast, Sassen (2004) contends that some global networks can "bypass" national authority rather than displace it. She argues for a highly specialized "denationalization" of certain institutional arenas in cities. Certain strategic sectors and functions in a city, such as banking and financial operations, are driven by economic globalization while the national system itself remains largely unaffected. From this perspective, globalization is embedded in a network of localities and some aspects of localities are involved in global transactions, demonstrating that both the global and the local are multi-scalar (Sassen 2004). Presumably those managing these global-local sectors are similarly denationalized, not to mention delocalized.

Some reterritorialization approaches fall under the rubric of "the new regionalism." Although "the new regionalism" can refer to a putative regional political agenda and coalition process (Brenner 2002), scholarly arguments about "the new regionalism" see the penetration of the state by market and international regimes as transforming territory and pushing regional actors to the fore (Keating 1998). In contrast to some early versions of the "hollowing out" argument, this is not a zero-sum process but a "rescaling and recomposition of European urban and regional governance" (MacLeod 1999). In Europe, it can occur through the problematic negotiations between EU institutions and local actors but also through efforts by the national government to establish metropolitan and regional institutions able to mobilize development assets to overcome uneven spatial development (see Newman 2000). The discourse on metropolitan governance in the U.S. and in Western Europe, especially, portrays metropolitan regions as the critical arena for promoting both local and national development prospects (Brenner 2002, 2003, 2004). In contrast to the administrative efficiency aspect of earlier metropolitan reform initiatives, contemporary projects emphasize the competitive and entrepreneurial features of regional economies. Localities within these regions cooperate in order to compete with other regions for investment.

As this suggests, regions are increasingly salient as investment sites and as sites for national and supranational policy initiatives as part of state restructuring processes. Brenner (2000) claims that national competitiveness increasingly is defined as contingent on construction of "Euro-regions" encompassing particular production activities, assets, and institutional configurations. To Brenner (1999) this re-territorialization process shifts economic regulation tasks to subnational levels as the national government devolves certain responsibilities in order to promote competitiveness and to accelerate adjustment to new economic forces. Although these arguments may seem to resemble the "Europe of regions" discourse, they generally assume some form of multi-level governance and continued national rule-making (John 2000). Swyngedouw (1997), for example, sees "glocalization" as a political process creating multiple layers of state authority and regulation and marked by conflict and contestation. Although a rather awkward term, "glocalization" captures the dialectical process by which global economic activities become more dispersed but also more embedded in particular territorial settings such as city regions, industrial districts and other such areas with "non-substitutable" locational assets (Swyngedouw 1997; Brenner 1998, 2002). By emphasizing the material and instrumental aspects of "the new regionalism," these authors remind us that power, ideology, and politics are part of these reterritorialization processes (Jouve and Lefèvre 2002; Peck and Tickell 1994). Rather than coherent and unified entities thrust into prominence by globalization forces, regions are "produced" through political struggles that are best understood through comparative research.

There is always the risk of reifying a particular scale – such as the region – as the object of study or seeing regions as privileged geographical arenas in a post-Fordist or globalizing economy (Brenner 2002). Indeed, Woods (2005) warns of "the scalar trap," a focus on the relative significance of different scales in shaping urban politics. In addition, there is the temptation to interpret the relation of the global and local in universal terms. The emerging reterritorialization orientation seeks to avoid this by challenging views of the local or the regional as constituted by geographic boundaries or nested scales. Its distinctly multi-scalar perspective underscores the importance of the relationships and linkages between scales. To the extent that these are shaped by new information technologies, localities become more integrated into global networks and local actors can link with other those in other localities and become part of global activist networks.

III. Accommodating the Global Context in Analyses of Local Processes

While the insights from directly theorizing global-local links are compelling, to date empirically grounded work to support and develop these ideas is slow to emerge. In particular, the emphasis on scales and ties does not easily accommodate notions of agency and autonomy (although see Swyngedouw 1997). Nor does the grand sweep of these arguments indicate a distinctive methodological strategy.

Empirical researchers face the daunting claim that globalization demands a "reformulation of past research paradigms" (Clark, 2000). While it is not necessarily the case that other approaches are "losing power" as Clark claims, it is clear they need to adapt to and incorporate these new conditions in order to maintain their robustness and explanatory power (Judge et al., 1995). In a sense, the concepts and frameworks in this second research literature approach global-local linkages "from the bottom up" – by identifying aspects of globalization processes that appear especially salient for internal policy making in cities and by sketching the evidence of diverse local responses to globalization trends (see Andersen and van Kempen 2001;

Bagnasco and Le Galés 2000; Le Galés and Harding 1998; Lidstrom 1999; Wyly et al. 1998). Four widely used constructs are discussed here in terms of their ability to explore local politics in the context of global-local links: regime theory, governance arrangements, cultural context, and policy agendas.

A. Regime theory/growth machines

Urban regime analysis is associated with Clarence Stone's (1989) study of Atlanta politics; it continues to be the dominant framework used for analysis of U.S. cities. In its most general meaning regimes refer to "the set of informal but relatively stable arrangements by which a locality is governed" (Stone 2002: 7). Within a political economy framework emphasizing the division of labor between market and state, it focuses on problems of collective action and political choice. The key issue is whether and how local public officials find ways of generating "enough cooperation" to get things done. They usually do so by developing informal arrangements that bring together those with strategic assets who share similar purposes and would also gain from more cooperation. In U.S. cities, this often but not always includes business interests; Stone (1989; 2005) consistently points out that there is no assumption that business participation is an essential attribute of a regime, only that regimes include those controlling the resources necessary for the capacity to act (see Brown 1999).

Given its roots in analysis of U.S. cities operating in a weak intergovernmental system and extremely dependent on private investment for revenues, some scholars question the adequacy of the regime concept beyond the American context (Davies 2004; Dowding 2001; Harding 1994). In short, can it travel? Are regimes appropriate characterizations of local politics elsewhere? (see Stoker and Mossberger 1994). Cobban (2003) argues No, not in the case of Canada. He contends that the regime concept is not useful for analyses of Canadian local politics because the structure and organization of more comprehensive municipal governments as well as regionally or nationally organized financial institutions in Canada alters the vulnerability of local politicians to local financial sector business elites. As a result, there is less incentive to cater to business interests in the diverse set of interests making claims on local decision makers. Wolfson and Frisken (2000), however, find that the devolution of many administrative and fiscal responsibilities to local municipalities in the Greater Toronto Area is encouraging the inter-municipal competitiveness characteristic of U.S. cities.

There is a growing consensus that changing conditions – such as local economic distress, European integration, enhanced global and intercity competition, political decentralization, changes in Socialist party ideology – are pushing local officials outside the U.S. towards economic and growth oriented priorities (Harding 1997, 1999). In the United States, Britain, and

France, Keating (1993) finds local politics being reconstituted, with the emergence of interclass, place-based development coalitions but mediated by national political factors. Similarly, Strom (1996) argues that patterns of federal support, the nature of the state bureaucracy, the prominence of architects, and the weak organization of the private sector have all shaped Berlin's approach to redevelopment.

Although there is some evidence of development-oriented local coalitions emerging in non-U.S. cities, they do not correspond to a single model; rather, they take differing forms in different national contexts with political and cultural characteristics influencing the nature of local coalition building (e.g. Levine 1993; John and Cole 1998). Nevertheless, the distributional consequences of these diverse forms may be similar: Logan et al. (1997) now contend that the most significant issue in analysis of growth machines is not the proliferation of growth coalitions but their distributional outcomes; as they skew local policy choices towards maximizing exchange values rather than use values, over time there are intensifying inequalities among places and the displacement of other policy priorities[3].

If we accept that regime concepts can be useful beyond the U.S. context, the question here is whether regime theory's emphasis on political leadership, coalition building, and policy choices is useful for analyzing local politics in a global era (Harding and Le Galès 1997). One issue is the extent to which the analysis of local regimes or coalitions is restricted to local actors. In the past, this has been more a matter of convenience, and perhaps disciplinary blinders, than a core component of the regime concept. Geographers (Cox 1997b; Cox and Mair 1988; Delaney and Leitner 1997) approach regimes as inherently multi-level coalitions engaged in the "politics of scale". As DiGaetano and Lawless (1999) point out, using regime concepts for comparative research requires greater attention to the effects of external forces and public-private interactions on regime formation.

Kantor and Savitch (2003) exemplify this dictum by using the regime concept to frame their comparative analysis of ten Western European and North American cities in terms of the interplay of local democratic development, market environments, and intergovernmental networks since the 1970s. They characterize globalization in terms of the international marketplace and ask how cities adapt and respond to these changing conditions. Structural

---

3   Regime theories and theories of the growth machine share similar concerns with the organization of power in cities. As developed by Logan and Molotch (1987), the sociological concept of growth machines emphasizes the interdependence of business and state power in land development; together these interests act as a "growth machine" pursuing their common interest in increased land values in a locality. Tensions between the use and exchange values attached to places generates local conflicts. Stone's (1989) concept of urban regimes recognizes this interdependence but is not limited conceptually to land development and encompasses a broader array of coalition partners. It is not unusual to see the distinctions between these approaches blurred.

factors, particularly intergovernmental structures, appear to influence critical aspects of local regime arrangements in these cities, particularly their governing coalitions, means of public-private coordination, and prevailing policy agendas on economic development. Their findings indicate that cities with stronger market positions in the international marketplace and embedded in more integrated intergovernmental systems are more likely to pursue social-centered policies. Not surprisingly, these are primarily European and Canadian cities. Cities with weaker market positions and more diffuse intergovernmental systems are more likely to pursue market-centered strategies. Again, not surprisingly these are primarily cities in the United States. But not all cities act accordingly: New York City, for example, weaves a course more frequently featuring social-centered policies than expected, thanks to the influence of its local political culture and vibrant processes of popular control.

Although there are many structural forces that may account more for a city's lack of success in the international marketplace than these local coalitions, the regime concept can be especially useful in assessing the failure to adapt to the global setting. Stone (2001) notes, for example, that Atlanta appears unable to move ahead on the new social problems presented by globalization and economic restructuring impacts. The biracial coalition or regime that figured so prominently in his original analysis now "shows signs of a declining ability to adapt to emergent issues and frame purposes accordingly." Similarly, Kantor and Savitch (2003) point out that Naples operates in a similar political and economic context as Milan yet is unable to muster effective policy responses to the changing global context. They attribute this to the pervasive clientelism hampering local government but also note, significantly, that a new reform mayor promises to mobilize public and private sector resources to change the image and the prospects of the city.

B. Governance

The regime concept clearly is amenable to multi-level analyses that take into account external influences shaping local choices although there are drawbacks in stretching the concept to cover an increasingly broad range of circumstances (Mossberger and Stoker 2001). But for some scholars (Cole and John 2001; DiGaetano and Strom 2003; DiGaetano and Klemanski 1999; DiGaetano and Lawless 1999; Harding 1994; Andrew and Goldsmith 1998; Bevir et al. 2003b), the governance concept is more useful for cross-national research than modified regime concepts.

Governance concepts represent a more abstract and general approach to local politics; the tradeoff is that we can not make the theoretical assumptions possible in a more precise concept such as regime. One marker of this imprecision, or evolving focus, is the expanding number of definitions of governance. Rhodes sees governance as "self-organizing, interorganizational networks characterized by interdependence, resource exchange, rules of the game and significant autonomy from the state." (Rhodes 1997: 15; 1996). Peter John suggests "Governance is a flexible pattern of public decision-making based on loose networks of individuals" (John 2001: 9). Some key attributes emerge across these definitions: governance networks are 1) self-organized, 2) loosely coupled, 3) interorganizational 4) interaction-units, which are 5) kept together because of their interdependency and 6) reciprocal trust and which make decisions on the basis of 7) negotiated agreements. (See also, Bevir et al. 2003a; Pierre 2000; Clarke 2005).

Peter John (2000) argues that globalization – or "internationalization" – pushes local governments towards local governance as they become involved in more complex and interdependent relations. Demands for greater private sector involvement in public decisions by business and nongovernmental actors are another pressure. Nearly every governance approach emphasizes that government is not enough in dealing with the collective action problems brought about by these processes. Different modes of governance are called into play to respond to collective action problems where actors seek mutual gains but must cooperate or coordinate their actions in the absence of hierarchy (Stoker 1998). Cox (1997a) reminds us that such collective action problems can be resolved by markets relying on price mechanisms, hierarchies using authority, or networks generating trust. Although these are analytically distinct, they do not operate alone; rather they overlap and interact, with governmental bureaucracies, for example, supporting networks.

Comparative analyses increasingly introduce governance perspectives in order to incorporate the role of intergovernmental and other external actors, although no one approach prevails. Local politics can be viewed as elements of intergovernmental structures in which the nation state shapes local governance arrangements. Some works take an institutionalist perspective on these relations, seeking to pinpoint the incentives and disincentives guiding local government choices. Note that Kantor, Savitch, and Haddock's (1997) analysis of eight cities in the U.S. and Europe emphasizes the bargaining environments created by intergovernmental systems, market positions, and local democratic practices. Sellers' (2002) comparative analysis of 11 European and North American cities extends this emphasis on "nested governance" by developing a typology of translocal institutional configurations to account for divergent local policy choices. The attributes of these institutional infrastructures are more significant in shaping local choices than substantive national policies, according to Sellers. In the context of a decentered national state and multi-level policy processes, globalization is taking place from below through "newly localized governance" processes (Ibid 377). In contrast, multi-level governance approaches see an intergovernmental focus as unnecessarily "state-centric;" instead they emphasize the importance of policy networks of decision makers and specialists that span policy domains and government levels (Marks 1996; John 2000). From this perspective, the "hollowing out" processes noted above denote vertical and horizontal shifts in governance, although the causal mechanisms are unclear (Van Hershberger and Van Warden 2004).

One of the core elements in governance analyses is the anticipation that new institutional arrangements are likely to emerge in manage the diverse players and interests (Mayer 1994). As Hirst (2000) puts it, governance arrangements "guide, steer, control or manage the wide range of new nongovernmental actors in civil society, and in the economy, to identify problems, exchange information and sometimes to jointly formulate and implement policies and programs." Many analyses of these arrangements use the regime and governance concepts interchangeably – an imprecision that hampers theory development[4]. The broad objective is to highlight coalitions and configurations of interests as well as the rules and institutions they develop in the governance process. Bullet (2002), for examples, traces the different "regimes of exclusion" in provision of social housing in German and English cities to the configuration of civil society and state associations in these cities along with the discourse of citizenship distinguishing the two settings. Nicholls (2003) develops the concept of "poverty regimes" to characterize the blending of public, private, and third-sector associations emerging in many European cities to take on new responsibilities for managing local poverty (see also Legalese 2002). He finds that incorporation of civil society associations into these efforts squelches their capacity to generate such democratic opportunities as mobilization, dissent, and participation. In both examples, the state framework proves decisive in shaping local policy choices.

Public private partnerships attendant to development issues are one of the most distinctive institutional mechanisms associated with governance (Modular et al. 2001). As Amin and Thrift (1995) point out, partnerships are one piece of a broader set of institutional changes attendant to globalization processes. They distinguish among places on the basis of "institutional thickness," a construct including partnership arrangements. Jon Pierre (1998) presents an institutionalist framework for making such comparative analyses of partnerships, applying it to cases in U.S. and European cities; similarly, DiGaetano and Strom (2003) analyze urban partnerships in the U.S., Great Britain, France and Germany. Davies' (2003) comparison of U.S. and U.K. partnerships is cautionary, arguing that the role of ideology and national initiatives makes the U.K. partnerships primarily symbolic. Unfortunately,

---

4   One distinction among these approaches is the regime theory focus on long-standing governing coalitions of business and political interests in contrast to the more fluid, multi-scalar, and broader scope of governance networks. Policy networks often refer to a more discrete set of decision processes and relations among public and private decisionmakers, sometimes characterized in terms of the centrality of the networks involved.

there is a tendency to conflate modes of governance with specific forms such as partnerships (Lowndes and Skelcher 1998) which hampers use of the governance concept.

While governance concepts seem promising means of capturing the more complex and interdependent global context in which localities operate, current conceptualizations slight power issues. Lefèvre (1998), for example, acknowledges the gains from viewing institutions as processes but questions whether the emphasis on internal aspects of governance arrangements slights the political and ideological dimensions of institution-building. Recent analyses of the impact of large-scale urban development projects (Geddes 2000), on social integration and polarization in European cities see this new governance as at the expense of traditional urban policymaking (Moulaert et al. 2001: 101). Indeed, it is panned as "planning for exclusivity," capturing public funds for large scale economic development projects at the expense of social concerns. Similarly, Le Galès (1998) argues for a more sociological conceptualization of governance, seeing cities as a level where different types of regulation are structured into governance arrangements.

C. Cultural Contexts

It is misleading to think about local politics in a global era without considering the cultural dimension. Globalization, transnational migration, and transnational activism potentially create more pluralistic, complex and autonomous local civil societies (Holston and Appadurai 2001; but see Nicholls 2003). Two dimensions are addressed here: the impacts of cultural globalization on local politics and the prospective shifts in values and culture related to the global spread of ideas and information.

The flow of people across borders and continents is a major dimension of globalization. Cities are the intersects of transnational flows of capital and people; as a result, immigration is an increasingly significant feature of local politics, posing new questions of citizenship, identity, and equality. Nearly every large and medium sized city in Europe and North America now hosts growing populations of recent immigrants from different cultural settings (Holston and Appadurai 1999). These groups engage in a "local politics of recognition" (Dusenbery 1999: 753) played out within different national frameworks – ranging from the explicit multicultural commitments of Canada, the United Kingdom, and other European governments to the more assimilationist stance of the U.S., France, and others. Although there are many nuances at the local level, recent debates over immigration in the U.S. tend to center on language and race as cultural markers whereas in Europe, and to some extent, in Canada (Dusenbery 1997) they center on religion (Zolberg and Long 1999: 7). Zolberg and Long attribute these distinctions to differences in national traditions rather than to the characteristics of immigration in the two settings. That is, European identity is embedded in a Christian tradition and the U.S. historically relied on language as a unifying element balancing other diverse cultural elements (Ibid). These religious and linguistic differences are "emblematic of the larger issues of inclusion and exclusion (Ibid, 28)." Along with other scholars (Soysal 1994) they anticipate different patterns of incorporation on linguistic, religious, and other cultural issues, reflecting the different institutional arrangements in which such issues are addressed. Indeed, one of the major intellectual questions is how race and ethnicity interact with other forms of stratification and identity such as gender and class. The prospects for the cultural dimensions of immigrant incorporation, therefore, depend on how negotiations of these differences and identities unfold at different scales.

Abu-Laban and Garber (2005) argue that the geography of immigration is socially constructed, leading to a "story" requiring national policy intervention in Canada but one depicting immigrant settlement patterns in the U.S. as an outcome of individual choices and therefore matters of local rather than national politics. In the U.S., many possibilities for boundary blurring— tolerance of multiple memberships and overlapping of collective identities (Zolberg and Long 9) – occur at the subnational level where decisions are made on bilingualism, voting in school board elections by non-citizen parents, and other cultural choices (Laws 1997; see Sharp 2005). Here cultural incorporation overlaps with the prospects for political incorporation. This underscores one of the critiques of a focus solely on civil society and cultural features – that state structures are significant factors in shaping civil society as well as the democratic possibilities therein (Nicholls 2003; Storper 1997).

A second cultural perspective anticipates shifts in values and culture related to the global spread of ideas and information. Tracking the "Europeanisation" of local governments, for example, demonstrates the steps by which ideas and working practices promoted by the EU begin to transform the management and core internal structures of local government (John 2000; Borraz and John 2004). In a more sweeping argument, Clark (2000) sees a new political culture emerging with globalization. Widespread shifts in values and cultural, including the spread of movements at the local level across Europe and North America, are hypothesized to be related to the global spread of ideas and information (Clark 2000; Clark and Hoffman-Martinot 1998; Clarke 2002). The new urban culture features more diversity, more citizen activism, greater attention to social issues and environmental concerns – post-material values. In line with the evidence of more entrepreneurial, development-oriented cities in Europe, Canada, and the U.S., both elites and citizens in this new local culture appear to place priority on fiscally conservative strategies but retain a commitment to broader social and environmental values as well. In this new political culture, the "rules of the game" are being redefined by these shifts in values. These culture shifts then prompt changes in local politics as well, including, potentially, the stronger styles of urban leadership emerging in some European cities (Borraz and John 2004).

Picking up on Soja's argument that we are moving away from a politics of equality to a "specifically cultural politics" centered on differences and identity, DeLeon and Naff (2004) systematically examine the prospects for a new political culture and identity politics in a multilevel comparative study of the United States and 30 urban communities. They find significant differences between the national and community samples in the importance of factors such as gender, race, class, and religion. Variations in local political cultures appear to significantly influence the importance of identity attributes such as race and religion in shaping political ideology, electoral behavior, and political protest. For their purposes, an index of socioeconomic place characteristics distinguishes the more traditional from the more nontraditional or innovative local political cultures[5]. Their findings demonstrate that "place matters" as a contextual and cultural influence on the strength and direction of relationships between social identity – particularly race and religion – and political outcomes in U.S. cities.

Globalization, culture, locality, and economic development also are linked in Richard Florida's (2002: 223) creative capital theory: "regional economic growth is driven by the location choices of creative people – the holders of creative capital – who prefer places that are diverse, tolerant, and open to new ideas." This argument directs our attention to the cultural milieus of specific localities, underscoring the importance of place for new economic sectors and for newly mobilized elites (See Scott 2000). Lewis and Rantisi's (2006) analysis of the design economy in Montréal traces the intricate governing mechanisms organizing this cultural industry, high-

---

5   The summative scale used as a New Political Culture (NPC) Index includes the percentages of each Social Capital Benchmark Survey community sample's total number of respondents on these seven items:
1. Secularism: % saying they adhere to no religion.
2. Nontraditional lifestyle: % who are unmarried.
3. Nontraditional gender roles: % classified as single working females.
4. Creative class: % classified as high on the SES Index : a 10 point scale with the highest rank indicating graduate education and more than $100,000 income.
5. Racial diversity and tolerance: % scoring a maximum of 3 on a Racial Diversity of Personal Friendships Index, constructed from the SCBS items asking about friendships with members of various racial groups. Index scores range from a low of 0 (no claimed personal friendships with any member of a different race) to a maximum of 3 (at least one personal friend in each of the three other racial groups).
6. Cultural diversity and tolerance: %saying they have a gay or lesbian as a personal friend.
7. Gay/lesbian presence: % who are unmarried, live with a partner, and say they have a gay or lesbian as a personal friend. This is a very rough proxy for the size of a community's gay and lesbian population. (cf. Florida's [2002, 255-56].

48

lighting the importance of nonprofit organizations and regulatory regimes in regulating cultural production. As the authors see it, promotion of the design economy in Montréal was, in part, an effort to promote Québec culture and cultural institutions in the face of increased cultural imports as well as to link cultural industries to economic development strategies. To Alan J. Scott (2006), these initiatives direct attention to the prospects for building creative cities and the possibilities for the emergence of a worldwide network of creative cities.

D. Policy Choices

Local policy choices are shaped by central-local relations, fiscal structures, party mechanisms, ideology and other structural features distinguishing local contexts (Andersen and van Kempen 2001; Bagnasco and Le Galés 2000; Goetz and Clarke 1993). Although cities may retain distinctive social, cultural, and political features in the face of globalization trends, it is possible that global competition could narrow the policy choices available to local policymakers[6]. That is, the pressures of global competition will lead to a convergence in local policy agendas privileging development priorities (see Clark 2000; Eisinger 1988; Peterson 1981; Rondinelli et al. 1998).

Many U.S. cities, of course, pursue such a course in response to their weak intergovernmental support and subsequent dependence on private capital investment (Peterson 1981). Donald (2005) argues that "scale politics" constrain Canadian cities' economic development strategies, with national government's reluctance to implement urban-based policies dampening local institutional change. Although European cities' greater integration with national policymaking systems makes policy convergence seem unlikely, David Harvey (1989) associates the displacement of city "managerialism" orientations by entrepreneurial policies with late capitalism rather than variations in intergovernmental structures. Peterson and Harvey's economic and political logics anticipate more entrepreneurial economic development strategies as a response to increased competitiveness; this encouraged many comparative analyses assessing whether this common goal elicits similar political dynamics. There is some cross-national evidence, for example, that mayors' spending preferences emphasize developmental policies (Saiz 1999). John and Cole's 1998 analysis of emerging developmental regimes in Leeds

---

6   Even within the market-oriented U.S. setting, a wide range of policy orientations are evident (Clarke and Gaile 1998; Walzer 1995); when the comparative analysis extends to European cities, where national and intergovernmental structures and party pressures exert powerful influence, a much more extensive set of policy choices is presented (Hudson 1993; Kantor et al. 1997; Garofoli 2002; DiGaetano and Klemanski 1993). Counter to Peterson, these orientations often feature more redistributionist and environmental priorities than anticipated; they can also vary in their attention to spatial and sectoral targeting.

UK and Lille, France builds on earlier work such as Michael Keating's (1991; 1993) comparison of local economic development politics in the U.S., Britain, and France. Savitch and Kantor's (2001) careful cross-national analysis of ten cities in five countries, however, reveals some local shifts toward more mercantile orientations but no consistent evidence of convergence in policy choices. They credit city-specific "steering factors" for this continued diversity: local political culture and the strength of popular control mechanisms influence the mix of social and market centered policies on local agendas.

But globalization and attendant economic changes may be reshaping local agendas in other ways. Globalization may be associated with more diverse local policy agendas – particularly the ascendance of consumption-oriented strategies such as the pursuit of entertainment and tourism dollars (Clarke 2002; Gladstone and Fainstein 2000; Judd and Fainstein 1999). This consumption orientation stems from the types of economic sectors and reterritorialization processes many scholars identify with globalization processes. For example, to the extent that well-off workers in these growth sectors, such as advanced producer services, seek consumption amenities, we can anticipate local agendas placing priorities on these features to attract such workers and firms. The role of consumption in local economies is a point of departure for absorbing analyses of the intersect of culture and politics in cities (Reichl 1999; Strom 1996).

IV. Globalization, Terrorism, and Localities

These theories and concepts of globalization and political change underscore the ways in which external forces alter the relative advantages of particular localities and the relative influence of interests within a community. Even though the consequences for particular localities and groups may be far from benign, globalization processes are seen as at least problematic in nature. Analytically, they can create opportunities as well as impose constraints. Not so with an increasingly significant aspect of globalization – terrorism.

There is growing scholarly analysis of the dark side of globalization – when cities become targets of terrorist attacks. All terrorism is local, ultimately (Clarke and Chenoweth 2006). Violence in cities is a longstanding historical pattern, including civil wars and social rebellions. Cities are "central venues of terror" (Savitch with Ardashev 2001): cities that are the seats of economic and political power historically serve as arenas for conflicts situated elsewhere. As centers of power, cities are sufficiently complex to hide terrorist movements and are magnets for media attention. Their very complexity, visibility, and interdependence make them vulnerable. The increasing use of the city for intentional and maximum impact attacks against local citizens forces the need to deal with terrorism onto many local agendas.

Recent terrorist attacks in the U.S. and Europe prompted scholars to see urban vulnerability in a broader, more proximate context. Indeed, Savitch (2003) contends that these trends – the diffusion of urban-based terror, the economic ramifications of urban terror, and the impact of terror on the use of urban space – constitute a new paradigm in which public security, order, and protection are now the central issues for cities. Many cities now confront what Savitch and Ardashev (2001) characterize as "tourism mixing along with terrorism." This is particularly so for global cities, such as New York City and London where tourism is a major economic sector and the impacts of terrorist attacks are magnified. Neill (2001) draws on the experiences of Belfast, Detroit, and Berlin to create a taxonomy of "marketing approaches in the face of fear," a new element in the economic development arena. Such efforts may well encourage the "tourist bubbles" that Judd observes in European and U.S. cities (Judd 1999), along with initiatives to "design out terrorism" by encasing public spaces in defensible materials (Coaffee 2004).

Paradoxically, the greater the national security threats, the more important the local role. Even in more centralized systems, national security policy is implemented at the local level so the local arena is the site where national security policies are adapted local needs. But in more decentralized Federal systems, as in the U.S., national security priorities initiatives often become refracted and diffused by local political dynamics. Local priorities, needs, and problems are wide-ranging and local officials set the agenda in response to local constituency concerns, which include security threats but are not limited to them (NLC 2002; Eisinger 2004). As a result, local policy responses are more variable even in the face of the threat of terrorism.

In the U.S. context, the local governance arrangements demanded by security agendas involve multiple stakeholders, reach across jurisdictions and bring together both public and private actors (Eisinger 2004; Savitch 2003; 2001; see also, Coaffee 2004). Each controls strategic resources necessary to "solve" the problem of hometown security. In this context, creating performance regimes for local security may be the most significant local governance issue (Clarke and Chenoweth 2006; see Stone 1998). Performance regimes or coalitions are driven and distinguished by a performance imperative, rather than the distributional benefits featured in most regime studies. This requires motivating stakeholders to make the outcomes – improved local security – rather than the processes or the perks, such as individual program budgets, buildings, or staff – the central concern. Constructing a performance coalition, therefore, is more than a matter of coordination: it involves developing a shared understanding of the problem and potential solutions and encouraging the active participation of diverse interests in collaborative activities focused on performance outcomes.

V. Globalization, Inequality, and Democratic Inclusion

One of the starkest consequences of globalization for local politics is the increasing inequalities associated with global competitive pressures. This is especially compelling in considering the problematic integration of new immigrants into subnational politics and community. The American literature tends to characterize the question of bringing marginalized groups into local political processes as a matter of political incorporation; stretching this concept to include recent immigrants is prompting reconsideration of the adequacy of the political incorporation concept itself. From a European perspective, immigrants and local politics are conceptualized in terms of social cohesion and social exclusion although this too is now under challenge.

A. Political Incorporation

Until recently, race and ethnicity has been a more central feature in U.S. urban studies than in Europe (but see Katznelson 1973). The concept of *political incorporation* is used widely in analysis of race and ethnicity in U.S. cities as well as, increasingly, in European cities. It looks beyond participation rates to assess whether racial and ethnic groups gain representation within the key governing institutions in government. Groups achieve political incorporation when their members become integrated into the governing coalition of a political jurisdiction. Representation is thus seen as a necessary, but not sufficient, condition for substantive influence. A pioneering series of comparative urban analysis of U.S. cities, now in its third decade, evaluates the changing degrees of political incorporation for African-American, Latino, and Asian residents (Browning, Marshall, and Tabb, 2003). Garbaye's comparison of Birmingham (UK) and Lille (FR) (2005) uses the political incorporation concept while emphasizing the importance of central-local relations, political parties, and local political processes in shaping the distinctive political incorporation patterns for ethnic minorities in each city. In Birmingham, these groups are incorporated into Labour party politics while in Lille, a powerful Socialist party machine excludes them. This suggests cross-national analysis of variations in styles or types of political incorporation of ethnic minorities is a promising research area.

The potential for coalitions among various ethnic/racial groups is another critical issue. A central theoretical question is under what conditions cooperation or competition would be anticipated between various groups. Regime theory sets out the conditions under which cooperation might occur, leading several scholars to consider the prospects for black-centered regimes (Reed 1995; Horan 2002; Orr and Walton 2001) as well as bi-racial or multi-ethnic coalitions and regimes (Hero 1992; Underwood 1997; Sonnenshein

1993). Stone's (2001) work on Atlanta analyzed the formation of a bi-racial regime centered on urban redevelopment; over time the regime's inability to come to a shared understanding on how to frame or define other problems led to its decline.

But recent waves of immigration have undermined the tendency to see U.S. politics "in black and white" (Lewis Mumford Center 2001) and increased the significance of race, ethnicity, and identity issues in European and Canadian cities. Subnational and local political arenas are where new immigrants and underrepresented groups are most likely to have the most immediate impacts occur, in the U.S. and in Europe and Canada, even though multiple layers of political power are involved in this process (Gerstle and Mollenkopf 2001; Jones-Correa 2001; Laws 1997). The political implications of these demographic and contextual changes are not clear, particularly if the links between ethnic and racial identity and political participation do not operate as in the past. Whereas immigrants and racial minorities historically used their ethnic identities and citizenship status to mobilize for local political incorporation in electoral politics, the contemporary arenas are more ambiguous (Bousetta 1996; 2000; Kim 1999; Jones-Correa 2005).

As in England, recent immigrants to the U.S. – and to some extent, resident African Americans and Latinos – often construct identities beyond the boundaries of the American nation state rather than within the context of American society alone. Recent research indicates immigrants in English cities, for example, may eschew traditional electoral politics but engage in issue-based activities that reach across cities and continents (ESRC 2003). This underscores the growing translocal nature of subnational politics in the face of territorially bounded democratic institutions in North American and European cities. In addition, the salience of electoral institutions for mediating the needs of underrepresented groups is diminished by the emergence of governance arrangements with multiple actors, agendas, and decision rules. And in the face of the growing importance of non-bureaucratic mechanisms for service delivery, a better understanding of the prospects for democratic inclusion when local government is only one of many players in local governance is necessary (see e.g. Hula and Jackson-Elmoore 2000; Mayer 1994; Mayer and Roth 1995).

As globalization pushes race, ethnicity, and identity politics to a more central position in North American and European cities, it is not clear that existing concepts – such as political incorporation – are adequate for examining situations where religion, language, and other 'non-racial' markers of difference may be more significant drivers of exclusion (ESRC 2004). Although race, ethnicity, and religion increasingly structure local political activities in a globalizing era, our theoretical frameworks for understanding these processes seem inadequate. Analyzing how groups construct their own identities rather than imputing interests to them based on socio-economic

53

characteristics is an important element of rethinking our approaches to race and identity in local politics (Keogan 2002; Zolberg and Long 1999). It is also important to understand how elites and institutional incentives frame and shape these identities (Croucher 1997). These lead us to more dynamic and interactive notions of incorporation, encompassing changes in the social, political, and economic structure of cities as well as in the immigrants and local citizens themselves (Zolberg and Long 1999)

B. Social Exclusion/Cohesion

As in the U.S., urban unemployment and poverty is a growing phenomenon throughout parts of European cities[7]. The coexistence of intra-urban areas of employment growth and high incomes with other intra-urban zones of high unemployment, low incomes and high dependence of welfare benefits has become increasingly common and seemingly long-term (Martin 1998). In European cities especially, EU and national urban policies can inject issues or broader policy orientations onto local agendas (e.g. Atkinson 2000; Davies 2003). Local social problems, for example, are drawing increased attention from the European Commission, the Organisation for Economic Co-operation and Development (OECD), and national governments in Europe. Issues such as social exclusion, human investment or immigration often involve regulatory mechanisms operating at multiple political levels (Atkinson 2000; Musterd and Ostendorf 1998).

But there is significant variation across European cities: van den Berg et al. (1997) compare the social strategies of eight cities in Finland, Sweden, Belgium, the Netherlands, and France and find that social policies are not defined in ways that allow integration with other policy sectors such as housing; furthermore, local organizing capacity for formulating and carrying out social policy varies greatly. Similarly, Geddes' (2000) analysis of 86 local partnership-based initiatives in 10 EU member-states aimed at promoting local development and social inclusion highlights the importance of funding from the EU and/or national policy programs. He points out that local partnerships are less likely to be inclusion coalitions capable of effective governance strategies for dealing with social exclusion. Indeed, local partnerships are associated with weak rather than strong discourses of social exclusion and inclusion: framing issues as solved by partnerships tends to foreclose the sphere of debate and action, excluding more radical options. Bulpett's (2002) comparison of welfare regimes allocating social housing in Southampton and Hamburg illustrates how different welfare regimes committed to similar objectives generate different policies of exclusion reflecting, in part, the

---

7   This section draws on Clarke and Walter-Rogg (2004).

ideological discourse on citizenship and larger welfare regimes in which they are embedded.

The use of "social exclusion" and "social cohesion" rather than "poverty" in Europe signals a significant redirection of policy attention from the material deprivation of the poor towards their ability to fully exercise their economic and political rights as citizens (Liebfried 1993; Geddes 2000; Atkinson 2000). This rhetorical distinction is subject to criticism, particularly to the extent that it actually obscures material inequalities and racial discrimination (Bulpett 2002) or suggests ahistorical and non-ideological developments (Moulaert et al. 2001). To Harloe (2001) and other critical theorists, the language of social inclusion is grounded in meritocratic assumptions and an emphasis on bringing in productive (as compared to non-productive) members of society. These terms also emphasize the fragmentation and isolation of newcomers to the city, with scant attention to the ways in which they come together to press for their priorities and agendas (LeGalès 2002). While exclusion and marginalization are persistent concerns, our analyses need to accommodate the processes by which immigrant groups become included in democratic practices at the local level.

C. The Challenges of Democratic Inclusion

The notion of democratic inclusion embraces the issue of unequally distributed citizenship rights (Crowley 2001). The pressures of globalization contribute to dilemmas of democratic inclusion by facilitating the transnational migration of culturally distinct groups to new communities and exacerbating material inequalities[8]. To the extent that we accept ethnicity, race, and culture as appropriate analytic categories and potential grounds for claims for representation (Crowley 2001: 107), many democratic inclusion issues at the local level are likely to center on the political incorporation of groups with distinctive nationalities and cultural identities. In Western Europe, ethnic political participation is characterized as "rather weakly structured and unstable" (Crowley 2001: 117). In the U.S., rates of naturalization and participation are low; in contrast to the pro-government activism and social initiatives promoted by bi-racial liberal coalitions in the past, there is some evidence that recent immigrant populations are more likely to support more moderate, pro-entrepreneurial orientations (Sonnenshein 2001: 215). These sentiments reflect an era of more limited government aspirations but also resonate with distinctive differences within and between Latino, African American, Asian, and white groups on social and economic issues. In both Europe and the U.S., democratic inclusion is contingent on particular

---

8   This section draws on Clarke (2005).

national and subnational institutional structures as well as group-specific attributes.

Focusing primarily on the characteristics of underrepresented groups and new immigrants overlooks critical changes in the urban context in which political incorporation and democratic inclusion processes operate. Representation and incorporation concepts assume a rather stable and consistent set of institutional arenas; they also traditionally focus on electoral mobilization and political incorporation aimed at making demands on the state. Neither condition can be assumed to be the case now in many communities. New types of participatory democratic practice, for example, are available to articulate new demands; for many groups, particular issues rather than group-specific interests drive their participation and these issues are not necessarily managed through state institutions. These features suggest rethinking our approaches to democratic inclusion to accommodate the changing local institutional landscape and to recognize the ways in which these institutions shape preferences as well as mediate demands.

VI. Conclusions

In responding to the initial question – whether the study of local politics is meaningful in a global age – we see a range of theoretical and conceptual arguments converging on the view that local politics itself is especially significant in a global era. World city and reterritorialization frameworks present cogent arguments about the vital economic roles played by subnational governments and governance arrangements. In "tying down" global forces and in constructing global ties through their interactions with other global and local organizations, localities become key architects of globalization.

This role makes understanding localities' internal political dynamics that much more critical. A variety of scholarly research strategies are available for analyzing these dynamics – regimes, governance, cultural tensions, policy agendas –. but all must now situate these internal dynamics as they now unfold in a new context of globalization. Issues of representation, participation, and responsiveness remain key concerns but how they are addressed under these new conditions is just beginning to be explored.

Given the relational and regional emphases emerging from the world city and reterritorialization approaches, crafting more nuanced and more context-specific analyses of local political dynamics seems appropriate. This does not argue against theory development but suggests more typological strategies, analyzing clusters of features or patterns as amenable to analysis and generalization. Creating typologies of global-local linkages, for example, would allow us to incorporate the historical context and to consider where and when these global-local linkages are historically-specific processes (White 1998). This promotes a move away from more structural, narrowly causal accounts to a more evolutionary analytic approach emphasizing contingent causality. Typological schemas would also encourage comparative analyses of political incorporation processes – particularly critical junctures and path dependent features of these processes – in cities sharing seemingly similar initial conditions and embarking on different paths toward democratic inclusion (Garbaye 2002; Lieberman 2001). In doing so, we can systematically determine how well these concepts and frameworks "travel" – to what extent are the theoretical, conceptual, and analytic vehicles we use context-specific or historically-bounded? This is one of the ongoing concerns in comparative research, a concern amenable to testing in considering global-local ties.

This overview indicates that localities and local politics are key sites for globalization and state restructuring but that traditional concepts and approaches may not be sufficient for analysis of local politics in a global age. It is imperative to both reconnect with basic political science concepts – power, representation, justice – and borrow from other disciplinary approaches. In many ways, scholars analyzing local political change were ahead of the political science discipline in recognizing and assessing the political impacts of globalization trends and processes. But it is fair to say that focusing only on the local level masked the relevance of many analyses for other levels of political activity. Similarly, the efforts to map out and understand these changing contextual features often drew scholars away from the core questions of political science. Firming the bridge linking analyses of local government and politics with political science theories and concepts is an especially important priority.

Drawing on theoretical frameworks and conceptual tools from other disciplines – especially geography, economics, and sociology – also will be essential for understanding these complex processes. Such borrowing and bridging promises mutual gain: economic and spatial arguments about global-local links often obscure issues of power and democratic practice; in some cases, they slight normative concerns with accountability, legitimacy, and representation as well. A more political orientation brings out the context-specific nature of many of these processes as well as their distributional consequences. But too often our analyses of local politics fail to take into account – in a systematic and precise way – the impact of these globalization trends and changing conditions on local politics. Our capacity to understand local politics in a global age is enhanced by bridging to core political science questions and borrowing from other disciplines.

References

Abu-Laban, Y./Garber, J.A. (2005): "The Construction of the Geography of Immigration as a Policy Problem: The United States and Canada Compared." Urban Affairs Review 40: 520-561.

Abu-Lughod, J. (1999): New York, Chicago, Los Angeles: America's Global Cities. Minneapolis: University of Minnesota Press.

Amin, A./Thrift, N. (1995): "Globalisation, Institutional 'Thickness' and the Local Economy." In: Healy, P./Cameron, S./Davoudi, S./Graham, S./Madani-Pour, A. (eds.): Managing Cities: The New Urban Context, pp. 91-108.

Andersen, H.T./Kempen, R.v. (eds.) (2001): Governing European Cities. Aldershot: Ashgate.

Andrew, C./Goldsmith, M. (1998): "From Local Government to Local Governance – and Beyond?" International Political Science Review 19: 101-117.

Atkinson, R. (2000): Combating Social Exclusion in Europe: The New Urban Policy Challenge. Urban Studies, vol 37. no. 5, pp. 1037-1055.

Bagnasco, A./Le Galés, P. (2000): Cities in Contemporary Europe. Cambridge U. Press.

Beauregard, R.A. (1995): "Theorizing the Global-Local Connection." In: Knox, P./ Taylor, P. (eds.): World Cities in a World System. Cambridge: Cambridge University Press: 232-48.

Beaverstock, J. V./Smith, R.G./Taylor, P. J. (1999): "A roster of world cities." Cities 16: 445-458.

Beaverstock, J.V./Doel, M.A./Hubbard, P.J./Taylor, P.J. (2002): "Attending to the World: Competition/Co-operation and Co-efficiency in the World City Network." Global Networks 2: 111-132.

Bevir, M./Rhodes, R.A.W./Weller, P. (2003a): "Traditions of Governance: Interpreting the Changing Role of the Public Sector." Public Administration 81: 1-17.

Bevir, M./Rhodes, R.A.W./Weller, P. (2003b): "Comparative Governance: Prospects and Lessons." Public Administration 81: 191-210.

Bliss, D. (2004): "Global Cities – Thinking beyond New York." Paper presented at the annual meeting of the Midwest Political Science Association Palmer House Hilton, Chicago, IL5.

Borraz, O./John, P. (2004): "The Transformation of Urban Political Leadership in Western Europe." International Journal of Urban and Regional Research 28: 107-20.

Bousetta, H. (2000): "Institutional theories of immigrant ethnic mobilisation: Relevance and limitations." Journal of Ethnic and Migration Studies 26: 229-245.

Bousetta, H. (1996): "Citizenship and Political Participation in France and the Netherlands; reflections on two local cases", New Community, 23(3), 215-231.

Brenner, N. (2004): New State Spaces: Urban Governance and the Rescaling of Statehood. Oxford: Oxford University Press.

Brenner, N. (2003): "Metropolitan Institutional Reform and the Rescaling of State Space in Contemporary Western Europe." European Urban and Regional Studies 10: 297-324.

Brenner, N. (2002): "Decoding the Newest 'Metropolitan Regionalism' in the USA: A Critical Overview." Cities 19: 3-21

Brenner, N. (2000): "The Urban Question: Reflections on Henri Lefebvre, Urban Theory and the Politics of scale." Symposium on Globalization, Politics and Scale, International Journal of Urban and Regional Research 24: 2.

Brenner, N. (1998): Global Cities, Glocal States: Global City Formation and State Territorial Restructuring in Contemporary Europe. Review of International Political Economy 5: 1-37.

Brenner, N. (1999): Globalisation as reterritorialisation: The re-scaling of urban governance in the European Union. Urban Studies 36: 431-451.

Brown, M. (1999): "Reconceptualizing Public and Private in Urban Regime Theory: Governance in AIDS Politics," International Journal of Urban and Regional Research 23: 70-87.

Bulpett, C. (2002): "Regimes of Exclusion." European Urban and Regional Studies 9: 137-149.

Cairncross, F. (2001): The Death of Distance. Cambridge MA: Harvard Business School Press.

Clark, T.N. (2000): "Old and New Paradigms for Urban Research: Globalization and the fiscal austerity and urban innovation project." Urban Affairs Review 36 (1): 3-45.

Clark, T.N./Hoffman-Martinot, V. (eds.) (1998): The New Political Culture. Boulder CO: Westview Press.

Clarke, S.E. (2005): "Splintering Citizenship and the Prospects for Democratic Inclusion." 2005. In: Wolbrecht, C./Hero, R.E. with Arnold, P.E./Tillery, A.B. Jr. (eds.): The Politics of Democratic Inclusion Philadelphia: Temple University Press. Pp. 321-362.

Clarke, S.E. (2002): "Globalism and Cities: A North American Perspective." In: Hambleton, R./Stewart, M./Savitch, H. (eds) (2002): Globalization and Local Democracy: A Cross-National Perspective. London: Macmillan, pp. 30-51.

Clarke, S. E./Chenoweth, E. (2006): "The Politics of Vulnerability: Constructing Local Performance Regimes for Homeland Security." Review of Policy Research 23: 95-114.

Clarke, S.E./Gaile, G.L. (1998): The Work of Cities. Minneapolis MN: University of Minneapolis Press.

Clarke, S.E./Walter-Rogg, M. (2005): "Emerging and enduring issues in the policy process." Presentation at the Fulbright/Odense University conference on "Developing a Comparative Urban Politics Curriculum." Odense, Denmark: May.

Coaffee, J. (2004): "Rings of Steel, Rings of Concrete and Rings of Confidence: Designing out Terrorism in Central London pre and post September 11th." International Journal of Urban and Regional Research 28: 201-211.

Cobban, T. (2003): "The Political Economy of Urban Redevelopment: Downtown Revitalization in London, Ontario: 1993-2002." Canadian Journal of Urban Research 12: 231-248.

Cole, A./John, P. (2001): Local Governance in England and France. Routledge.

Cox, K. (1997a): "Governance, Urban Regime Analysis, and the Politics of Local Economic Development." In: Lauria, M. (ed.): Reconstructing Urban Regime Theory: Regulating Urban Politics in a Global Economy. Thousand Oaks CA: Sage, pp. 99-121.

Cox, K.R. (1997b): Spaces of Globalization New York: Guilford.

Cox, K.R./Mair, A. (1988): "Community and locality in the politics of local economic development." Annals of Association of American Geographers 78 (2) 307-325.

Croucher, S. (1997): Imagining Miami. Charlottesville VA: University Press of Virginia.

Crowley, J. (2001): "The Political Participation of Ethnic Minorities." International Political Science Review 22: 99-121.

Cumbers, A./MacKinnon, D./McMaster, R. (2003): "Institutions, Power and Space." European Urban and Regional Studies 10: 325-342.

Davies, J.S. (2004): "Can't Hedgehogs be Foxes too? Reply to Clarence N. Stone." Journal of Urban Affairs 26 (1), 27-33.

DeLeon, R./Naff, K.C. (2004): "Identity Politics and Local Political Culture: Some Comparative Results from the Social Capital Benchmark Survey." Urban Affairs Review July.

Delaney, Da./Leitner, H. (1997): "The Political Construction of Scale." Political Geography 16: 93-97.

DiGaetano, A./Strom, E. (2003): "Comparative Urban Governance: An Integrated Approach." Urban Affairs Review, 38: 356-396.

DiGaetano, A./Klemanski, J.S. (1999): Power and City Governance: Comparative perspectives on urban governance. Minneapolis and London: University of Minnesota Press.

DiGaetano, A./Lawless, P. (1999): "Urban Governance and Industrial Decline: Governing Structures and Policy Agendas in Birmingham and Sheffield, England, and Detroit, Michigan, 1980-1997," Urban Affairs Quarterly 34: 546-557.

Donald, B. (2005): "The politics of local economic development in Canada's city-regions: New dependencies, new deals, and a new politics of scale." Space and Polity 9: 261-281.

Dowding, K. (2001): "Explaining Urban Regimes," International Journal of Urban and Regional Research. Vol. 25, No. 1 (March), 7-19.

Dusenbery, V.A. (1997): "The Poetics and Politics of Recognition: Diasporan Sikhs in Pluralist Politics." American Ethnologist 24: 738-762.

Eisinger, P. (1988): The Rise of the Entrepreneurial State. Madison WI: University of Wisconsin Press.

Eisinger, P. (2004): "The American City in an Age of Terror: Preliminary Assessment of the Effects of 9/11." Urban Affairs Review 40: 115-130.

Economic and Social Research Council (ESRC) (2004): "Ethnicity: division or cohesion? New challenges in a changing world." Programme Proposal Under Development.

Economic and Social Research Council (ESRC) (2003): "Ethnic Minorities Opt For Issue-Based Campaigns Rather Than Party Politics," September 24: Press Release.

Evans, P. (2002): Livable Cities: Urban Struggles for Livelihood and Sustainability. Berkeley: University of California Press.

Evans, P. (1997): "The Eclipse of the State? Reflections on Stateness in an Era of Globalization." World Politics 50: 62-87.

Florida, R. (2002): The Rise Of The Creative Class. New York: Basic Books.

Friedmann, J. (1986): "The World City Hypothesis." Development and Change, 17: 69-83.

Friedman, J. (1995): "Where We Stand." In: Knox, P./Taylor, P. (eds.): World Cities in a World System. Cambridge: Cambridge University Press, Appendix and Chap. 2.

Gabriel, O.W./Hoffmann-Martinot, V./Savitch, H.V. (eds.) (2000): Urban Democracy. Opladen: Leske + Budrich.

Garbaye, R. (2002): Ethnic minority participation in British and French cities: a historical-institutionalist perspective. International Journal of Urban and Regional Research 26: 555-570.

Garbaye, R. (2005): Getting Into Local Power. London: Blackwell.

Geddes, M. (2000): Tackling Social Exclusion in the European Union. International Journal of Urban and Regional Research 24: 782-800.

Gerstle, G./Mollenkopf, J. (eds.) (2001): E Pluribus Unum? Contemporary and Historical Perspectives on Immigrant Political Incorporation. New York: Russell Sage Foundation.

Gladstone, D.L./Fainstein, S.S. (2000): "Tourism in US Global Cities: A Comparison of New York and Los Angeles." Journal of Urban Affairs 23: 23-40.

Goetz, E./Clarke, S. E. (eds.) (1993): The New Localism: Comparative Urban Politics in a Global Era. Newbury Park, CA: Sage.

Guidry, J./Kennedy, M./Mayer, Z. (eds.) (2000): Globalizations and Social Movements: Culture, Power, and the Transnational Public Sphere. Ann Arbor: University of Michigan Press.

Hambleton, R./Stewart, M./Savitch, H. (eds) (2002): Globalization and Local Democracy: A Cross-National Perspective. London: Macmillan.

Hamel, P./Lustigger-Thaler, H./Mayer, M. (eds.) (2000): Urban Movements in a Globalizing World. London: Routledge.

Harding, A. (1994): "Urban Regimes and Growth Machines: Toward a Cross-National Research Agenda," Urban Affairs Quarterly 29: 356-382.

Harding, A. (1997): "Urban Regimes in a Europe of Cities," European Urban and Regional Studies, vol. 4, 4, 291-314.

Harding, A. (1999): 'Review Article: North American urban political economy and British research.' British Journal of Political Science, 29: 673-98.

Harding, A./Wilks-Heeg, S./Hutchins, M. (2000): 'Business, government and the business of urban governance.' Urban Studies 37: 975-94.

Harding, A./Le Galés, P. (1997): "Globalization, urban change and urban policies in Britain and France." In: Scott, A. (ed.): The Limits of Globalization. London: Routledge. Chapter 8.

Harloe, M. (2001): "Social Justice and the City: the new 'liberal formulation'." International Journal of Urban and Regional Research 25: 889-897.

Harvey, D. (1989): "From Managerialism to Entrepreneurialism: The Transformation in Urban Governance in Late Capitalism," Geografiska Annaler 71B: 3-17.

Held, D. (1999): "The Transformation of Political Community: Rethinking Democracy in the Context of Globalization." In: Democracy's Edges Cambridge: Cambridge University Press.

Hill, R.C./Kim, J. (2000): "Global cities and developmental states." Urban Studies 37: 2167-2198.

Hill, R.C./Fujita, K. (2003): "The Nested City." Urban Studies 40: 207-217.

Hill, R.C. (2004): "Cities and Nested Hierarchies." International Social Science Journal. 56: 373-384.

Hirst, P. (2000): "Democracy and Governance." In: Pierre, J. (ed.): Debating Governance: Authority, Steering, and Democracy. Oxford: Oxford University Press, pp. 13-35.

Holston, J./Appadurai, A. (2001) : Introduction. In: Holston, J. (ed.): Cities and Citizenship. Durham, NC: Duke University Press. pp. 1-17.

Hula, R.C./Jackson-Elmoore, C. (2000): Nonprofits and Urban America. Westport CT: Greenwood Publishing.

Jessop, B. (1997): "The Entrepreneurial City." In: Jewson, N./MacGregor, S. (eds.): Transforming Cities: Contested Governance and New Spatial Divisions. London and New York: Routledge. 28-41.

Jessop, B. (1998): "The Rise of Governance and the Risks of Failure." International Social Science Journal 155: 29-45.

John, P. (2000): "The Europeanisation of Sub-national Governance." Urban Studies, 37(5-6): 877-894.

John, P. (2001): Local Governance in Western Europe. London: Sage.

John, P./Cole, A. (1998): "Urban Regimes and Local Governance in Britain and France: Policy Adoption and Coordination in Leeds and Lille." Urban Affairs Review 33: 382-404.

Jones-Correa, M. (2005): "Bringing Outsiders In: Questions of Immigrant Incorporation." In: Wolbrecht, C./Hero, R.E. with Arnold, P.E./Tillery, A.B. Jr. (eds.): The Politics of Democratic Inclusion, Philadelphia: Temple University Press.

Jones-Correa, M. (2001): "Structural Shifts and Institutional Capacity: Possibilities for Ethnic Cooperation and Conflict in Urban Settings." In: Jones-Correa, M. (ed.): Governing American Cities: Inter-Ethnic Coalitions, Competition, and Conflict. New York: Russell Sage Foundation.

Jouve, B./Lefèvre, C. (2002): Urban Power Structures: Territories, Actors and Institutions in Europe. In: Jouve, B./Lefèvre, C. (eds.): Local Power, Territory and Institutions in European Regions (pp. 7-34). London: Frank Cass.

Judd, D. (1999): "Constructing the Tourist Bubble." In: Judd, D.R./Fainstein, S.S. (eds.): The Tourist City, New Haven: Yale University Press. Pgs. 35-53.

Judge, D./Stoker, G./Wolman, H. (1995): Theories of Urban Politics. London: Sage.

Kantor, P./Savitch, H.V. (2003): Cities in the International Marketplace. Princeton, N.J.: Princeton University Press.

Keating, M. (1998): The New Regionalism in Western Europe. Cheltenham: Edward Elgar.

Keating, M. (1993): "The Politics of Economic Development: Political Change and Local Development Policies in the United States, Britain, and France," Urban Affairs Quarterly vol. 28, no. 3

Keating, M. (1991): Comparative urban politics: Power and the city in the United States, Canada, Britain, and France. Aldershot, UK: Edgar Elgar.

Keogan, K. (2002): "A sense of place: The politics of immigration and the symbolic construction of identity in Southern California and the New York metropolitan area." Sociological Forum, 17 (2): 223-253

Kim, C.J. (1999): "The Racial Triangulation of Asian Americans." Politics and Society 27: 105-138.

Knox, P. (1995): "World Cities in a World-System." In: Knox, P/Taylor, P. (1995): World Cities in a World System. Cambridge, Chap 1.

Laws, G. (1997): "Globalization, Immigration and Changing Social Relations in U.S. Cities," Annals of the American Academy of Political and Social Science 551 (1997), pp. 89-104.

LeGalès, P. (1998): "Regulations and Governance in European Cities." International Journal of Urban and Regional Research 22, 4: 550

LeGalès, P. (2002): European cities, social conflict and governance. Oxford University Press

LeGalès, P./Harding, A. (1998): "Cities and States in Europe," West European Politics, vol. 21, 3 (July), pp. 120-45.

Lefèvre, C. (1998): "Metropolitan government and governance in western countries: a critical review." International Journal of Urban and Regional Research 22: 1: 26.

Levi, M./Olson, D. (2000): "The Battles in Seattle." Politics and Society 28: 309-329.

Levine, M. (1993): "The Transformation of Urban Politics in France: The Roots of Growth Politics and Urban Regimes," Urban Affairs Quarterly vol. 29: 383-410.

Lewis, D./Rantisi, N.M. (2006): "Governing the Design Economy in Montreal, Canada." Urban Affairs Review 41: 309-337.

Lewis Mumford Center for Comparative Urban and Regional Research (2001): Metropolitan Racial and Ethnic Change – Census 2000. http://mumford1.dyndns.org/

Lidstrom, A. (1999): The Comparative Study of Local Government Systems – A Research Agenda. Journal of Comparative Policy Analysis: Research and Practice 1: 97-115

Liebfried, S. (1993): "Towards a European Welfare State? On integrating poverty regimes into the European Community." In: Joes, C. (ed.): New Perspectives on the Welfare State in Europe. London: Routledge

Logan, J./Molotch, H. (1987): Urban Fortunes. Berkeley: University of California Press

Logan, J. R./Rhaley, R. B./Crowder, K. (1997): "The Character and Consequences of Growth Regimes: An Assessment of 20 Years of Research," Urban Affairs Quarterly vol. 32, no. 5

Lowndes, V./Skelcher, C. (1998): "The Dynamics of Multi-organizational Partnerships: An Analysis of Changing Modes of Governance." Public Administration 76: 313-333.

MacLeod, G. (1999): "Place, Politics and 'Scale Dependence': Exploring the Structuration of Euro-regionalism." European Urban and Regional Studies 6: 231-254.

Marks, G. et al. (1996): "Competencies, cracks and conflicts: Regional Mobilization in the European Union." In: Marks, G. et al. (eds.): Governance in the European Union. London: Sage.

Martin, R. (1998): Regional dimensions of Europe's unemployment crisis. In: Lawless, P./Martin, R./Hardy S. (ed.): Unemployment and Social Exclusion. Landscapes of Labour Inequality. London, Jessica Kingsley, p. 11-48.

Martinotti, G./Pozzi, C. (2004): "From Seattle to Salonico (and beyond): Political tourism in the second generation metropolis." Presented to City Futures International Conference, Chicago, Il, 8-10 July.

Mayer, M. (1994): "Post-Fordist City Politics." In: Amin, A. (ed.): Post-Fordism: A Reader (316-337). Oxford and Cambridge: Blackwell.

Mayer, M./Roth, R. (1995): "New Social Movements and the Transformation to Post-Fordist Society," In: Darnovsky, M./Epstein, B./Flacks, R. (eds.): Cultural Politics and Social Movements. Philadelphia: Temple University Press, pp. 299-319.

McNeill, D. (1999): "Globalization and the European City." Cities v. 16, n.3: 143-148.

Mossberger, K./Stoker, G. (2001): "The Evolution of Urban Regime Theory: The Challenge of Conceptualization," Urban Affairs Quarterly 36: 810-835.

Moulaert, F./Swynedouw, E./Rodriguez, A. (2001): "Social Polarization in Metropolitan Areas: The role of new urban policy." European Urban and Regional Studies 8: 99-102.

Musterd, S./Ostendorf, Wim (eds.) (1998): Urban Segregation and the Welfare State: Inequality and Exclusion in Western Cities. London: Routledge.

National League of Cities (NLC) (2002): Homeland Security and America's Cities. Research Brief on America's Cities. Washington DC: National League of Cities

Neill, W.J.V. (2001): "Marketing the Urban Experience: Reflections on the Place of Fear in the Promotional Strategies of Belfast, Detroit and Berlin." Urban Studies 38: 815-828.

Newman, P. (2000): "Changing Patterns of Regional Governance in the EU." Urban Studies 37: 895-908.

Nichols, W.J. (2003): "Poverty Regimes and the Constraints on Urban Democratic Politics: Lessons from Toulouse, France." European Urban and Regional Studies 10: 355-368.

Peck, J./Tickell, A. (1994): "Searching for a New Institutional Fix: the After-Fordist Crisis and the Global-Local Disorder." In: Amin, A. (ed.): Post-Fordism: A Reader. Oxford: Basil Blackwell. 280-315.

Peterson, P. (1981): City Limits. Chicago: University of Chicago Press.

Pierre, J. (2000): "Models of Urban Governance. The Institutional Dimension of Urban Politics." Urban Affairs Review 34: 372-396.

Reichl, A.J. (1999): Reconstructing Times Square: Politics and Culture in Urban Development Manhattan KS: University Press of Kansas.

Rhodes, R.A.W. (1996): "The New Goverance: Governing without government." Political Studies 44: 652-67.

Rhodes, R.A.W. (1997): Understanding Governance: Policy Networks, Governance, Reflexivity and Accountability. Buckingham: Open University Press.

Rondinelli, D.A./Johnson, J.H. Jr./Kasarda, J.D. (1998): " The Changing Forces of Urban Economic Development: Globalization and City Competitiveness in the 21st Century." Cityscape 3: 71-105.

Saiz, M. (1999): "Mayoral Perceptions of Developmental and Redistributive Policies: A Cross-National Perspective," Urban Affairs Review 34: 820-842.

Sassen, S. (2004): Denationalization: Economy and Polity in a Global Digital Age. Princeton, NJ: Princeton University Press.

Sassen, S. (2001): Cities in a World Economy. Thousand Oaks, CA: Pine Forge Press.

Sassen, S. (1996): "Cities and Communities in the Global Economy: Rethinking our Concepts," American Behavioral Scientist 39: 629-39.

Sassen, S. (1991): The Global City: New York, London, Tokyo. Princeton, NJ: Princeton University Press.

Savitch, H.V./Ardashev (2001). "Does Terror Have an Urban Future?" Urban Studies 38: 2525-2533.

Savitch, H.V. (2003): "Does 9-11 Portend a New Paradigm for Cities?" Urban Affairs Review, 39: 103-127.

Scott, A.J. (2006): "The Creative City: Conceptual Issues and Policy Questions." Journal of Urban Affairs 28: 1-16.

Scott, A.J. (2000): The Cultural Economy of Cities. London: Sage.

Scott, A.J./Agnew, J./Soja, E.W./Storper, M. (2001): "Global city-regions." In: Scott, A.J. (ed.): Global City-Regions: Trends, Theory Oxford: Oxford University Press. P. 11-29.

Sellers, J.M. (2002): Governing from Below. Cambridge University Press.

Sharp, E. (1999): Culture Wars and Local Politics. Lawrence KS: University Press of Kansas.

Smith, M.P. (1998): "The Global City – Whose Social Construct Is It Anyway?" Urban Affairs Review, 33: 482-48.

Smith, M.P. (2000): Transnational Urbanism. London: Blackwell.

Sonnenshein, R.J. (2001): "When Ideologies Collide, What's a Leader to Do? The Prospects for Latino-Jewish Coalition in Los Angeles." In: Jones-Correa, M. (ed.): Governing American Cities: Inter-ethnic Coalitions, Competition, and Conflict. New York: Russell Sage. Pgs. 210-229.

Soysal, Y. (1994): Limits of Citizenship. Chicago: University of Chicago Press.

Strom, E. (1996): "In Search of the Growth Coalition: American Urban Theories and the Redevelopment of Berlin." Urban Affairs Quarterly 31: 455-481.

Stoker, G. (1998): "Governance as Theory: Five Propositions." International Social Science Journal 155: 17-28.

Stoker, G./Mossberger, K. (1994): "Urban Regime Theory in Comparative Perspective", Government and Policy, 12, 195-212.

Stone, C. (1989): Regime Politics: Atlanta. Lawrence, KS: University Press of Kansas.

Stone, C.N. (1998): "Introduction: Urban education in political context." In Changing Urban Education, Clarence Stone, ed. Lawrence, KS: University Press of Kansas.

Stone, C. (2001): "The Atlanta Experience Re-examined: The Link Between Agenda and Regime Change." International Journal of Urban and Regional Research 25: 20-34.

Stone, C. (2005): "Looking Back to Look Forward: Reflections on Urban Regime Analysis." Urban Affairs Review 38:1-33.

Storper, M. (1997): The Regional World: Territorial Development in a Global Economy. New York: Guilford Press.

Swyngedouw, E. (1997): Neither Global Nor Local: 'Glocalisation' and the Politics of Scale. In: Cox, K. (ed.): Spaces of Globalization: Reasserting the Power of the Local. (pp. 137-166). New York/London: Guilford/Longman.

Taylor, P.J. (2004): "Regionality in the world city network." International Social Science Journal 56: 361-37.

Van den Berg, L.J./van der Meer, P.M.J. Pol. (2003): "Organising Capacity and Social Policies in European Cities." Urban Studies 40, 10: 1959-1978.

Van Kersbergen, K./Van Waarden, F. (2004): "'Governance as a Bridge Between Disciplines: Cross-disciplinary inspiration regarding shifts in governance and problems of governability, accountability and legitimacy." European Journal of Political Research 43: 143-171.

Vetter, A. (2000): "Democracy in Big Cities: The Comparative View." In: Gabriel, O. W./Hoffmann-Martinot, V./Savitch, H.V. (eds.): Urban Democracies, Opladen: Leske + Budrich, S. 433-452.

White, J.W. (1998): "Old wine, cracked bottle? Tokyo, Paris, and the global city hypothesis." Urban Affairs Review 33 (March): 451-477.

Wolfson, J./Frisken, F. (2000): "Local Response to the Global Challenge: Comparing Local Economic Development Strategies in a Regional Context." Journal of Urban Affairs 22: 361-384.

Wood, A. (2005): "Comparative urban politics and the question of scale." Space and Polity 9: 201-215.

Wyly, E.K./Glickman, N.J./Lahr, M.L. (1998): "A Top Ten List of Things to Know About American Cities." Cityscape, 3: 7-32.

Zolberg, A.R./Long Litt Woon. (1999): "Why Islam is Like Spanish: Cultural Incorporation in Europe and the United States." Politics and Society 27: 5-38.

Chapter 3
Methodologies and Research Methods in Urban Political Science

Peter John

Local political systems have much in common with those at other levels of governance, particularly the national level. In most democratic countries, political parties run candidates to seek office in local government; local decisions emanate from a well-defined executive structure; a deliberative chamber of elected representatives debates and makes decisions on the issues of the day; policies are administered by a permanent bureaucracy; interest groups seek to influence public decisions; and the citizens participate, to a greater or lesser extent, and consume the policy outputs that local governments produce. With such a common set of political features, it is no surprise that the methodologies and research methods that have been used by political scientists to study these aspects of politics at the national level have been applied to local government and to its political cultures.

And there is nothing wrong with standardisation. To the extent that political science has a universal claim to knowledge, it is reasonable to expect urban political scientists to apply general theories and to test familiar models. For example, urbanists have tested hypotheses that follow from sociological models of politics to find out who participates in the policy process (e.g. Clark 1968a); and they have investigated the extent of bureaucratic autonomy as formulated by the principal-agent-model (Stein 1990). It is also consistent with this line of argument that theories may be developed or adapted for the urban context, and then taken up and applied in other parts of the political system, though this direction of theory travel is not as common as the other way round. The main examples of the upward route are usually quite old, the main one being the methods and techniques used to study the exercise of power. Community power studies of the 1960s (cf. Dahl 1961, Polsby 1963) influenced the study of other jurisdictions during the subsequent forty years (see the review by Dowding 1996). Latterly, the regime concept, which has been used to analyse informal coalitions of public and private policy-makers (Stone 1989), finds its echo in studies of national and international regimes, though it is very difficult to find cross-citations. Social capital, on the other hand, did make its first outing at the sub-national level, with Putnam's (1995) research that correlated levels of voluntary membership and policy-performance of Italy's elected regional governments. Even with the massive boom across many policy fields and disciplines, social capital research depends on levels of networks, trust and volunteering to be different across space, so that local government, with its in-built control of institutional design and room for autonomy for policy-makers, creates a natural research opportunity for researchers to test the impact of social capital as well as to find out about its origins (e.g. see Smith et al. 2000).

It is likely that the typical urban politics research project deploys the same research instruments as the rest of political science, seeking to meet the highest standards of inference, and aiming to use valid data that may be replicated (cf. King et al. 1994). Studies of local electoral behaviour, for example, apply standard techniques for evaluating and testing public opinion, using data from surveys and/or real events and/or population characteristics, and testing models using descriptive statistics and multivariate techniques, such as Miller's (1988) study of the local influences on voting behaviour and Kaufmann's (2004) analysis of group conflict in urban elections. Political scientists frequently employ surveys to examine local decision-makers, such as bureaucrats (e.g. Mouritzen and Svara 2002) and councillors (e.g. Welch and Bledsoe 1988). Then there are the voluminous case studies that use the ubiquitous methods of interviewing, collecting secondary sources and interpreting data. Indeed, a textbook on methods in urban research, *Doing Urban Research*, is really a compendium of established practices in social science rather than an exegesis of those particular to the urban context (Andranovitch and Riposa 1993). The solid advice to students of urban politics must be that they take general methods courses, such as on survey analysis, time series techniques and research design. Nobody can argue with the claim that good political science methods are good urban ones too.

Whilst the main assumption of this chapter is that general methodologies and methods apply to the study of urban politics, there are two features of urban politics that allow researchers to develop techniques or at least forms of analysis that are not so common in the rest of the discipline: *numerosity* and *propinquity*. The claim of this chapter is that, in general, urban political scientists do not proclaim methods that use these aspects of local political systems, but just do them or hint at them in their research, for which a reference to M. Jourdain's prose-speaking abilities would be apposite if it were not so hackneyed a phrase! The message here is that urban political scientists could trumpet more what they do, and they could be less dependent on other methods in political science.

Numerosity

Numerosity is the multiple occurrences of local governments within nation states, which can come to many hundreds for some European countries and thousands for the United States of America. The abundance of cases is of course small when compared to the individuals who participate or not in politics, so they do not usually reach the numbers in surveys measuring public opinion. But compared to other units of political analysis that political scientists wish to generalise about, in particular the institutions of the nation state, where there is often only one case, there are usually a reasonable number of sub-national units from which to make generalisations. Large numbers confer advantages because, when a time series of data points is not available, they permit conventional statistical analysis to take place on instItutional forms and behaviour, and also on policy occurrences and outcomes. Even with a cross-sectional design, data using sub-national governments as the cases usually has numbers that are sufficiently large to justify standard parametric tests (statistical tests that draw on the random properties of large numbers) rather than techniques that need to deal with the properties of smaller numbers, such as bootstrapping, applied in situations where there are relatively few cases as, for example, in studies of the politics of the US states (Mooney 1997). The impact of leadership forms, performance of institutions, and effects of institutional design can be tested in ways that are not usually possible or straightforward at the national level. One example is the Welch and Bledsoe study (1988) cited earlier; another is Gains et al.s (2005) appraisal of the differential and path-dependent impact of the institutional reforms in England in 2000, where the research performs statistical tests on different institutional forms using a sample of all English local governments.

There are many studies using the classical techniques of statistical analysis, which have sub-national units as the cases. In contrast to surveys of individuals where the dependent variable is often nominal, such as the party the individual wishes to vote for, urban data often has intervals as the gradation, because the dependent variable can easily turn into a percentage or score within the local unit, which make the use of the traditional multivariate research technique, ordinary least squares (OLS), a routine occurrence. One example is the relationship between population size of local government and democratic performance as measured in per cents for each jurisdiction (e.g. Gaardsted 2002). Another uses surveys of mayors to test hypotheses about responses to fiscal austerity (Clark and Furguson 1983). Such analysis is very difficult with national or cross national-level data, where the number of oganisations or countries can be very small or hard to generalise across, such as between different federal agencies.

Few articles in the mainstream political science units use such a naturally occurring set of units of political organisation, whereas typically the small number of countries available for analysis, such as 21 in the Organisation for Economic Cooperation and Development (OECD) are deployed extensively. With such small numbers, researchers are unable to know if the assumptions of OLS regression have been breached or not. How is it possible to test for normal or random distribution of the dependent term with so few cases, as for example in Castles and Merrill's (1989) use of causal regression techniques on OECD country cases? The alternative is to pool the data over time and space and to use new techniques for analysis of variation on both these dimensions. But the statistical properties of pooled cross-sectional case design are not yet fully understood. For example, comparative political economy specialists have used these panels to test the idea that left-leaning governments with particular forms of political support can maintain welfare spending (Alvarez et al. 1991). But the estimation technique was criticised by Beck and Katz (1995); and even these experts' conclusions have in turn been questioned on statistical grounds (Plumper 2004, Kittell and Winner 2005). Political scientists are keen to reward innovations rather than applications of 'bog-standard' techniques, but if state of the art means falling foul from a lack of numbers, perhaps it does not always pay off? The numerous local output studies, testing for the effects of parties and other variables on budget outcomes, face no such problems (e.g. Sharpe and Newton 1984, Boyne 1996). After all, one of the big advantages of OLS is that, with sufficient cases, its properties and assumptions are very well understood. Most users know when the underlying assumptions have been breached, and what to do if they are. How often do analysts using, for example, multinomial probit, report checks for breaches of the assumptions of their models? In contrast, checks for the standard problems of multicollinearity and heteroscedasticity are routine for publications using OLS.

Large numbers do not mean just routine analysis. Urban researchers have pioneered analysis that captures the statistical properties of spatially distributed cases. One of the best examples of innovative methods is Clarke and Gaile (1998), who seek to find out how autonomous cities are in the face of environmental constraints, having at their disposal a dataset that allows regression analysis, which is impossible to carry out at the nation state level, which tends to keep to descriptive statistics (see Hirst and Thompson 1999) or uses the pooling procedure discussed above. Clarke and Gaile deploy trend surface analysis, which is a statistical technique that has been developed by geographers to sort out the causal connections in the data and to allow for spatial effects. The contiguity of spatial units may lead to a breach of the assumption of independence of the observations, and thus has particular application to many situations in urban politics, where what happens in one jurisdiction can affect what happens in a neighbouring one. With the use of GIS software and a greater understanding of spatial autocorrelations, there is now a sub-field on spatial models in urban politics, though appearing more in geography-focused publications (e.g. Gimpel et al. 2004) rather than in political science ones. Spatial autocorrelation may not just be a feature of urban politics, but could occur in any analysis where non-randomly selected spatial units are the cases, such as countries in the same region of the world or electoral districts within a nation state. This problem is rarely discussed within mainstream political science, which would make a methodological contribution from the problems of the urban field of general interest. Urbanists can use other related innovative techniques, such as ecological inference, which is the analysis of aggregate data, often collected at the subnational or juridisdictional level.

Propinquity

The second characteristic of urban politics is propinquity, which denotes the closeness of urban political and social actors to each other and to the social processes that affect localities, which occurs because of the relatively small size of the urban space when compared to other decision-making units. This means that many of the key actors know each other in a local elite network of key bureaucrats, party people, and media personnel, and where local political institutions are not as differentiated as they would be at the national level. This integration of key actors and institutions can generate much flexibility in urban decision-making, which comes from micro-level personal interactions that affect how the political game operates (Yates 1977), a closed form of politics that often attracts critiques from radicals and leftists. The propinquitous character of local politics partly explains why social network approaches have been popular (Hunter 1953; Galaskiewicz 1979; John 1998). Though these close and intricate relationships can be drawn using sociometric or network data techniques, often the best way of analysing them is through the single case study, based on a series of semi-structured interviews with key participants, essentially qualitative pieces of research, sometimes using some quantitative data to enhance the analysis. For this reason, there are numerous case studies of local decision-making, most of them are based on one case, and often exploring a particular theoretical framework through the interviews. Some of these studies have already been mentioned, such as the elite studies like Hunter's (1953) study of Chicago, then the pluralist studies of the 1960s and 1970s (Dahl 1961; Banfield 1961), and the UK single city studies, for example of Birmingham (Newton 1975). In spite of some valiant attempts to develop systematic large-N analysis to test for community power structures (Clarke 1968b), the 1970s and 1980s saw more single place studies in the Marxist tradition (e.g. Saunders 1980) and then in the influential regime theory analysis, applied in Atlanta (Stone

1988), in Dallas (Elkin 1987), and then across the US and in Europe (see John 2001 for a review). Given the importance of networks, case studies allow the researcher to 'soak and poke' their research subjects (cf. Fenno 1978, p. xiv) to see if what is observed fits within the theoretical paradigm. Repeated interviews are feasible, particularly as urbanists often live and work next to their research site in their city or region, which puts them at a massive advantage compared to, for example, their colleagues who work on international relations issues, through of course they are many urbanists who study cities and localities in other countries from their own. Typically the urban researcher will get to know the local city, build up relationships with local elites, often encouraged by economic development-minded universities keen to promote their role in the local community. These relationships then become key human resources for research projects, where the urbanist can explore the local dimension of a particular theoretical orientation. Typically, local political institutions will commission research from universities, which can be used to inform case-orientated urban research, usually based on a limited selection of interviewees, using the comments made in semi-structured interviewees to inform the argument being made. In that sense the propinquity of urban politics extends to the urban researchers themselves.

Many single case studies, such as by Dahl (1961) and Stone (1989) have become classics in a way that would not be predicted by standard social science methods. As Rogowski (1995) demonstrates, many path-breaking studies are often based on one case, such as the book that launched consociational studies (Lijphart 1968), which was based on the observation of success of elite accommodation in the Netherlands, a dramatic example of selection bias. In turn, the classic urban studies have inspired other researchers to look at single cases, which partly explains the profusion of studies. Single case studies are compelling because the reader can probe the case alongside the researcher, making it more immediate and memorable than a statistical compendium. While few of these studies discuss the limitations of and potential for bias in the single case design, they make claims about the exercise of power or existence of regimes, which may apply elsewhere. There is rarely an attempt to develop a common methodology. While researchers do valid things, such as examine variation within case studies, interview as wide a range of actors as possible, both in-group and out-group ones, and seek to observe change over time, the reader is reliant on the judgement and intuitions of the author about the validity of the research rather than methods that would meet the replication standard.

The second dimension of propinquity is that the impacts of decisions are more readily observable to those who govern localities, and also are more easily seen in the researchers' own eyes, than those coming from higher levels of governance (Yates 1977). The conditions of cities or localities in terms of social and economic problems, race relations, unemployment and pollution, are part of both the elites and researchers' immediate experiences, and one aspect of the research problem is about looking at the links between elite perceptions and policy problems in the same spatial scale. This aspect of local politics also encourages the use of certain sort of methods, in particular those that are attune to the intentions of policy-makers and help understand their experience of their contexts. Hence interviews, which probe the aims of policy-makers, and in depth studies that examine the implementation of policy decisions involving 'street-level' bureaucrats, are common in urban political analysis. Indeed, some urbanists would like to be or are anthropologists.

Partly because of these concerns, and from more general intellectual movements, researchers in fields such as social policy and the environment tend to adopt a critical stance toward the dominant scientific paradigms in social science, which assumes an objective reality that can be measured and quantified. Instead they are sympathetic to critical paradigms that seek to limit the oppressive gaze of the researcher, and embrace the perspectives, language and autonomy of those who are being researched. Thus qualitative techniques aim to record the voice of the human subject and to break down the potentially distorting and one-sided relationship between the researcher and the researched. Qualitative urban researchers sometimes believe there is a similarity between the scientific methods dominant in political science and the ways in which powerful actors, such as bureaucrats, elites and politicians, tend to govern localities through rational techniques, with a strong distinction between the rulers, who govern and use the rational techniques of government, and the ruled who are subject to objective interventions from the rulers. Urbanists, by being both critical of the techniques of government and the methods of so-called positivist social science, seek to break potentially oppressive relationships between governors and governed on the one hand and researcher and researched on the other. They are 'bottom up' in their assessment of methods and of urban political systems. For example, there is research on gender and the city that uses alternative perspectives on public problems and is critical of the way in which conventional and 'neutral' public policies hide more inclusive interests and perspectives (Booth et al 1996).

The comparative potential

It might seem that numerosity and propinquity generate different types of research designs; one statistical and inferential; the other qualitative and interpretative, each deferring to well established research paradigms. But such divisions are mainly stereotypes, and indeed it is possible to have integrated research designs that make best use of both characteristics. Here we find the comparative logic behind effective social science is particularly useful in the study of urban politics. In particularly, the comparative case study can use numerosity to select cases so as to ensure focused comparisons, where cases can be selected on the basis of extreme examples, or typical cases or cases where one variable is held constant. At the same time, these studies can also be based on the closeness and integration of urban systems to make inferences from within the case as well as across it.

Comparative work often works well within countries. The project by Stone (1998) on regimes and education policy used nine locations to compare and contrast what works, using largely qualitative insights into the cases. Ferman (1996) compares Chicago and Pittsburgh in depth to explain difference processes and outcomes. Another regime example is Dowding et al's (1999) comparative qualitative analysis of six regimes at the borough level in London to test hypotheses about regime formation and performance. Similarly on regimes, Kilburn (2004) compares fourteen US cities. What distinguishes this piece of research is a careful attention to selection of cases through the secondary literature with the aim of comparing different types of regime, and ascertaining the formation of coalitions through the careful description and comparison of cases. The author uses Qualitative Comparative Analysis (QCA), a method elaborated by Ragin, which is a technique somewhere between qualitative and quantitative analysis allowing the research to examine and count the particular configuration of features of a case that may lead to the outcome of interest. Finally, it is possible to combine in the same study a survey with a large number of observations and complementary case studies of a small number of authorities, which can reap the advantages of careful case selection and large N. Thus Reese and Rosendfield (2002) deploy what they call a 'blended methodological approach', where they used quantitative methods in a survey of 305 Canadian cities and 682 US ones, which was used for analysis of the content of local economic development policies. The data was used to select nine cities with different leadership models and civic cultures to test the hypotheses about what affects policy outputs and outcomes.

However, within-country variations will only offer a limited quasi-experimental range because many of the key variables of institutions and cultures differ within strict parameters, which may mean limited variation in key independent or dependent variables. When considered across countries these key variables vary, making the challenge to control for some urban features such as city size and industrial structure. One of the most powerful features of sub-national analysis is its ability to compare both countries and local governments in the same research design (see Denters and Mossberger 2004 for a review of this argument). This procedure overcomes the main disadvantage of studies in traditional comparative politics – that of small numbers – and also adds variation within the nation state, which increases the ability to generalise.

In this manner, sub-national observations can be very useful in comparative country research because it stops researchers over-generalising from a one-country case (Snyder 2001). Snyder argues that sub-national units allow the researcher to observe the spatially varied dimensions to global and other processes. This reasoning is close, though not quite at the core of urban political science, for an urban political scientist would resist solely being an underlabourer for comparative scholars, producing cases to improve the main aim of explaining country variation. Instead the urbanist regards the city or locality as the primary focus, and then examine other levels of government as further elaborations of the explanation. It is the city, in its critical role as in the interface of political, social and economic interactions, that is in the vanguard of global economic processes, which are also mediated through national structures and power bases. What the comparative method allows is for some clustering of observations within the nation states to observe differences between localities and then compare causes and effects across nation states.

In recent years, more comparative research designs have grown common, partly in reaction to the internationalisation of research problems through economic competition and social changes, such as migration, that affect the urban space in comparable ways. Stronger research networks are playing their part, encouraging fruitful collaborations. In general, comparative local research is not fully developed, with the majority of US urbanists selecting cases within their county. In Europe, the main stress has not been methodological but descriptive of different trends, with the common format as the edited collection from country experts addressing a common theme (e.g. Sharpe 1993), a format that still dominates the field (e.g. Denters and Rose 2005), partly because it is relatively easy to produce. It is possible to overcome the collective action problem of producing such volumes, for example the anticipation of the pace of the slowest contributor, by providing low-cost selective incentives, such as an invitation to a workshop in a country with a pleasant climate and timed to coincide with writing deadlines. Because the cost is low, these volumes tend contribute little to knowledge, being mainly literature reviews and containing descriptions. Indeed, one of the reasons for the lack of methods-driven cross-national comparative research is the sheer difficulty of carrying it out. For the lone researcher, it involves costly travel, the learning or refinement of languages to a level so local elites can be interviewed; which can restrict the number of countries that can be covered; for the cross-national team there are the classic collective action or coordination problems as research teams expand, which means that projects can crash because of a team from one country does not deliver by attempting to free-ride or just being inefficient or misunderstanding the research design. Then there is the near impossibility of organising timely co-funding from different national funding streams, which again means that the successful comparative projects tend to focus on two or three countries, limiting the ability to test hypotheses. The larger projects tend to be run on a shoestring (e.g. FAUI), and thus depend on goodwill rather than the power of resources to implement successfully a common research design.

The most common are comparisons of one case from each country, often testing out ideas that cities respond differentially to the international economy. For example, the world cities literature examines the role of these centres in the world hierarchy of cities (e.g. Gordon et al. 1992). Of more methodological promise is the incorporation of variations between localities at the same time as places are being compared across countries. Savitch and Kantor, for example, take three cities in the US, one in Canada, two in France, two in the UK, and two in Italy. They allow the cases to vary by economic conditions, central-local relationships and politics to generate inferences. John and Cole (1998; 2001) use the most-similar-most-different method to generate inferences by selecting two pairs of cities that are similar across countries, which are very different institutionally, to examine whether networks are similar and different in two contrasting policy sectors of education and economic development. Returning to regimes, which seem to have stimulated more comparative work than other subtopics, DiGaetano and Klemanski (1999) compare two cities in the US with two in England to compare governing regimes. The most methodologically developed qualitative piece, and one that also uses quantitative evidence, is Sellers' (2002) comparison of eleven medium cities in France, the US and Germany in response to globalisation of the economic context for policy policy-making. What distinguishes this volume is the minute attention to detail which builds to generate inferences of a powerful kind. Again, there is the good use of the numerous cases of local governments across jurisdictions and countries, with attention to the contingent relationships within each case.

There are less studies using large numbers in comparative analysis. However, this kind of analysis is too often rarely achieved or carried out, partly because of the costs of collecting data systematically across countries, also because it is hard to measure the variables in a consistent manner, particular where there different sizes of jurisdiction and different institutional rules and structures. A good example is Aiken et al's (1987) comparison of metropolitan systems – 76 in France, 83 in Italy, 74 in Germany, and 63 in England and Wales – by correlating expenditure with population sizes, and then regressing number of headquarters, the population size of the hinterland, employment-residence ratio, the percentage of the Labour force in services and measures of the prevalence of left politics on the operating expenses of central cities. The comparative insights came from comparing the regression coefficients on identical equations for each country.

More quantitative in character is the use of surveys and/or other aggregate data from a representative sample of municipalities, such as in the Fiscal Austerity and Urban Innovation (FAUI) project, where Clark extended his surveys of US political elites to a common model across most countries in the world, which allowed for the testing of hypotheses of the emergence of new forms of politics, relating to political parties, post-modernisation and populism, but were the incidence differs massively according to country context (e.g. Clark et al. 1985;Mouritzen 1992; Clarke 1989; Clark 1994; Saiz and Geser 1999; Clark and Hoffman-Martinot 1998). Another is the use of surveys of elites in a smaller number of countries, such as the Jacob et al (1971) study of the impact of local factors on leadership across four countries. Then there is the Mourizen and Svara (2002) surveys of chief executives in 14 European, North American and Australasian countries, and the Jacob survey of municipalities in four countries cited above. Similarly, the Elderveld et al's (1995) study of local elites' attitudes surveys mayors, council members, department heads and party leaders in 55 middle-sized cities in the USA, Sweden and the Netherlands. Likewise, Rose (2002) examines whether variation in the population size of municipalities has an effect on differences in the levels of local non-electoral participation taking survey evidence from Denmark, the Netherlands and Norway. Denters (2002) analyses levels of trust in local governments in Denmark, the Netherlands, Norway and the United Kingdom.

Many of these studies emerge from fortuitous collaborations and the availability of already existing and comparable survey data to test certain hypotheses. Indeed, most of the citations are multi-author in contrast to the one-author single case studies of earlier years. More ambitious research would engage in more comprehensive data collection. The problem is the effort and care needed to gather comparative and comparable data. The best example to date is 'Sellers' (2004) unpublished paper, which uses aggregate data to test out hypotheses concerning the link between the infrastructure of local government and the type of welfare state. A number of scholars are converging in their interest in these kinds of local government issues, and new data sources and tests are likely to emerge as the twenty-first century progresses.

Conclusions

There is much to celebrate in the methodologies and research methods used in urban political science. Given the heterogeneity of urban issues and the variety of types of scholars, it is not surprising that a variety of methods appear in the journals, both qualitative and quantitative, which address a number of policy and academic issues. There is a pleasing diversity, which reflects the cross-currents of change in the urban space and the different kinds of academics that study it. Geographers, sociologists, social policy specialists as well as political scientists find the politics of the urban space fascinating. Indeed, interdisciplinarity is one of the great strengths of urban analysis. As a result there is a plurality of methods and perspectives used to understand these phenomena, which reflect different academic traditions. In general, however, urbanists tend to use the methods that come to hand within their disciplines and backgrounds, and reproduce standard kinds of analysis.

The central argument is that what makes urban politics unique within the discipline of political science is two characteristics of what is being studied: one is the relatively large numbers that exist, which gives rise to reliable and valid statistical analysis as well as interesting and focused case study designs; the other is close integration of urban systems, which can encourage in depth and sympathetic qualitative analysis. The logic of the argument presented here is that urban political scientists need not just draw on conventional methods in the rest of political science, but can use the possibilities for comparative case design to increase leverage over the problems that are studied at the local level, which also have wider applicability in the rest of political science, drawing on both numerosity and propinquity as drivers of urban research methodologies and methods. In some works, it is possible to select examples of interesting cases to observe; in others, the integration is caused by comparing in-depth cases studies to generate intellectual leverage both within and across the cases. The most productive avenue for such an integrated approach is comparative urban political analysis, with variation within and across nation states, both using large numbers and with qualitative dimensions. So far there are few examples of such blending of research designs, but there are some signs that the promise of urban political analysis is about to be realised through the plan for a new section of the American Political Science Association on comparative urban politics. More comparative research may help urban political science contribute to methodological knowledge rather than just receive it.

References

Aiken, M. (1987): 'Urban systems theory and urban policy: a four-nation comparison', *British Journal of Political Science,* 17: 341-358.
Alvarez, R./Garrett, G./Lange, P. (1991): 'Government partisanship, labor organisation, and macroeconomic performance', *American Political Science Review*, 85: 539-56.
Andranovitch, G./Riposa, G. (1993): *Doing Urban Research* London: Sage.
Banfield, E. (1961): *Political Influence.* New York: Free Press, 1961
Beck, N./Katz, J. (1995): 'What to do (and not to do) with time-series cross-section data', *American Political Science Review* 89 (3): 634-647.
Booth, C./Dark, J./Yeandle, S. (1996): *Changing Places. Women's Lives in the City.* Paul Chapman Publishing.
Boyne, G. (1996): Constraints, Choices and Public Policies. London: JAI Press.

Castles, F./Merrill, V. (1989): 'Toward a general theory of public policy outcomes'. (1989) *Journal of Theoretical Politics*, 1, 177-212.

Clark, T. (1968a): 'Community structure, decision-making, budget expenditures, and urban renewal in 51 American communities; *American Sociological Review*, 33 576-593.

Clark, T. (ed.) (1968b): *Community Structure and Decision-Making*. San Francisco and Chicago: Chandler/SRA

Clark, T. (ed.) (1994): Urban Innovation: Creative Strategies in Turbulent Times. London: Sage.

Clark. T./Ferguson, L. (1983): *City Money*, New York, NY: Columbia University Press.

Clark, T./Hellstern, G.-M./Martinotti, G. (eds.) (1985): *Urban Innovations as Response to Urban Fiscal Strain*. Berlin: Europäische Verlag.

Clark, T./Hoffmann-Martinot, V. (eds.) (1998): *The New Political Culture*, Boulder: Westview.

Clarke, S. (1989): Urban Innovation and Autonomy: The Political Implications of Policy Change. London: Sage.

Clarke, S./Gaile, G. (1998): *The Work of Cities*, Minneapolis: University of Minnesota Press.

Dahl, R. (1961): *Who Governs?* New Haven: Yale University Press.

Denters, B. (2002): 'Size and political trust: evidence from Denmark, the Netherlands, Norway and the United Kingdom'. *Environment and Planning C: Government and Policy* 20: 793-812.

Denters, B./Mossberger, L. (2004): *Methodological issues in comparative local politics*, contribution to the Fullbright Comparative Urban Politics syllubus project, coordinated by Clarence Stone.

Denters, B./Rose, L. (2005): *Comparing Local Governance* Basingstoke: Macmillan.

DiGaetano, A./Klemanski, J. (1999): *Power and City Governance Comparative Perspectives on Urban Development,* University of Minnesota Press.

Dikec, M. (2004): 'Social movements and globalization', *International Journal of Urban and Regional Research*, 28: 713-716.

Dowding, K. (1996): *Power.* Buckingham: Open University Press.

Dowding, K./Dunleavy, P./King, D./Margetts, H./Rydin, Y. (1999): 'Regime politics in London local government. *Urban Affairs Review* 34: 515-45

Eldersveld, E./Stromberg, L./Derksen, W. (1995): *Local Elites in Western Democracies*. Boulder, Colo.: Westview.

Elkin, S. (1987): *City and Regime in the American Republic.* Chicago: University of Chicago Press.

Fenno, R. (1978): *Home Style.* Boston: Little, Brown and Company.

Ferman, B. (1996): *Challenging the Growth Machine*. Lawrence: The University Press of Kansas.

Gaardsted, F. (2002): 'Size and electoral participation in local elections', *Environment and Planning C: Government and Policy*, 20 : 853-869.

Gains, F./John, P. C./Stoker, G. (2005): 'Path dependency and the reform of English local government; *Public Administration,* 83(1), 22-45.

Galaskiewicz, J. (1979): 'The structure of community organizational networks', *Social Forces* 57 (4): 1346-1364.

Geddes, B. (2004): *Paradigms and Sand Castles.* Ann Arbor: University of Michigan Press.

Gimpel, J./Morris, I./Armstrong, D. (2004): 'Turnout and the local age distribution: examining political participation across space and time', *Political Geography*, 23: 71-95.

Gordon, I./Fainstein, S./Harloe (1992): *Divided Cities: New York and London in the Contemporary World*. Blackwell.

Hirst, P./Thomspon, G. (1999): *Globalization in Question*, 2nd edition. Cambridge: Polity Press.

John, P. (1998): 'Urban economic policy networks in Britain and France; a sociometric approach', *Environment and Planning C: Government and Policy*, 16, 307-322.

John, P. (2001): *Local Governance in Western Europe*. London: Sage.

John, P./Cole, A. (2001): *Local Governance in England and France*. London: Routledge.

Hunter, F. (1953): *Community Power Structure*. Chapel Hill: University of North Carolina Press.

Jacob, P. (1971): *Values and the Active Community*. New York: The Free Press.

Lijphart, A. (1968): The Politics of Accommodation. Pluralism and Democracy in the Netherlands. Berkeley: University of California Press.

Kaufmann, K. (2004): The Urban Voter: Group Conflict and Urban Voting in American Cities. Ann Arbor: University of Michigan Press.

Kilburn, H.W. (2004): 'Explaining U.S. urban regimes: A Qualitative Comparative Analysis', *Urban Affairs Review*, Vol. 39, No. 5, 633-651.

Kittell, H./Winner, H. (2005): 'How reliable is pooled analysis in political economy? The globablization-welfare state nexus revisited', *European Journal of Political Research*, 44(2).

King, G./Keohane, R./Verba, S. (1994): *Designing Social Inquiry*. Princeton, NJ: Princeton University Press.

Miller W. (1988): Irrelevant elections? The Quality of Local Democracy in Britain. Oxford: Clarendon Press.

Mouritzen, P.-E. (ed.) (1992): *Managing Cities in Austerity*. London: Sage.

Mouritzen, P.-E./Svara, J. (2002): *Leadership at the Apex*. Pittsburg: Pittsburg University Press.

Mooney, C.Z. (1997): *Monte Carlo Simulation*. Newbury Park, CA: Sage

Polsby, N. (1963): *Community Power and Political Theory*. New Haven, CT: Yale University Press, pp. 122- 138.

Putnam, R. (1995): *Making Democracy Work*. Princeton: Princeton University Press.

Newton, K. (1975): *Second City Politics*. Clarendon: Oxford.

Plumper, T./Troeger, V./Manow, P. (2004): 'Panel analysis in comparative politics: Linking method to theory', *European Journal of Political Research*, forthcoming.

Reese, L./Rosenfeld, R. (2002): *The Civic Culture of Local Economic Development*. London: Sage.

Rogowski, R. (1995): 'The role of theory and anomaly in social science inference', *American Political Science Review*, 89: 467-470.

Rose, L. (2002): 'Municipal size and local non-electoral participation: findings from Denmark, the Netherlands and Norway. *Environment and Planning C: Government and Policy* 20: 829-52.

Rose, L. (2002): 'Municipal size and local non-electoral participation: findings from Denmark, the Netherlands and Norway. *Environment and Planning: Government and Policy* 20: 829-52.

Saiz, M./Geser, H. (eds.) (1999): *Local Parties in Organizational Perspective.* Oxford: Westview Press.

Saunders, P. (1980): Urban Politics: A Sociological Interpretation Harmonsworth, Penguin.

Savitch, H./Kantor, P. (2002): The Political Economy of Urban Development in North America and Western Europe. Princeton: Princeton University Press.

Sellers, J. (2002): *Governing from Below.* Cambridge: Cambridge University Press.

Sellers, J. (forthcoming): 'Local government and the egalitarian welfare state', Governance.

Sharpe, L. (ed.) (1993): *The Rise of Meso Government in Europe,* London: Sage.

Sharpe, L./Newton, K. (1984): *Does Politics Matter?* Oxford: Oxford University Press.

Smith, G./Maloney, W./Stoker, G. (2000): 'Social capital and urban governance: adding a more contextualised 'Top-Down' perspective', *Political Studies,* 48: 4, 802-820.

Snyder, R. (2001): 'Scaling down: The subnational comparative method', *Studies in Comparative International Development* 36 (1): 93-110.

Stein, R. (1990): 'The budgetary effects of municipal service contracting: a principal-agent explanation', *American Journal of Political Science,* 34: 471-502.

Stone, C. (1989): *Regime Politics: Governing Atlanta, 1946-1988.* Lawrence: University Press of Kansas.

Stone, C. (ed.) (1998): *Changing Urban Education.* Lawrence: University of Kansas Press.

Welch, S./Bledsoe, T. (1988): *Urban Reform and its Consequences* Chicago: University of Chicago Press.

Yates, D. (1977): *The Ungovernable City.* Cambridge: MIT Press.

Chapter 4
The Infrastructure of Research and Academic Education[1]

Vincent Hoffmann-Martinot

This chapter presents an overview of the infrastructure of research that has evolved for the support of local government studies in political science since the 1970s. We shall successively deal with national research institutions, international scientific networks, and finally information and publication resources. The emphasis of the presentation is on research centres and networks that pursue a predominantly political science oriented agenda, although some institutions of a more multi-disciplinary nature will also be mentioned.

National Traditions and Institutions

Research centres and academic departments

Basic infrastructure units of research and academic education in the field of local government studies are represented by political science research centres and academic departments. They usually comprise competent teams and individuals, research libraries, databases, consultancy capacities, and are, in brief, poles of specialized research. We shall not consider the many academic institutions where no more than one or two experts work on issues related to local politics. In fact, in most countries the institutions that display a substantial research infrastructure in this field are fairly few in number.

For a long time local government studies were likely to be more developed and better endowed in decentralized countries like the United States or Switzerland where sub-national politics and policies historically were key issues in the analysis of the national political system. But this contrast has largely faded since the 1980s under the impact of decentralization/regionalization reforms throughout a number of traditionally centralized countries like

---

1 This contribution has greatly contributed from comments and improvements provided by my dear colleagues Harald Baldersheim and Hellmut Wollmann

France, Israel, or Spain. In the latter countries, a new and strong interest in local affairs has spawned often impressive institutionalization of various teaching and research initiatives focusing on the previously neglected world of local government.

One could reasonably expect that the stronger the level of or the trend towards decentralization and the more professionalized the political science community in a given country, the more developed its research infrastructure in local politics. The respective influence of the two conditioning dimensions is of course extremely variable according to the chosen national context. It is, for instance, clear that the still weak development of the discipline of political science in China or in Arab countries largely explains the quasi-absence of specialized research centres in these regions of the world. On the other hand it is all the more surprising to observe that in the Federal Republic of Germany, one of the leading countries in the early development of political science, resources and infrastructures for local government studies are still today relatively limited.

The most spectacular "boom" of research capacities is likely to happen in democratizing nations that (re-)discover the virtues of local government no longer strictly dominated by central authorities, like the former communist systems of Central and Eastern Europe, or in several African, Latin American, and Asian countries where national but also foreign institutional actors (governments, foundations, international organizations in particular) are keen to foster the development of local civicness and decentralized governance. "Good governance", the catchword intended to combine the master objectives of democratization of local political systems and professionalization of public management, has driven huge assistance programs towards many Southern countries. Here, research activities appear to be often closely interwoven with practices of "democratic learning", while the need to assess results precisely has created a demand for new social sciences research bodies.

There are obviously striking differences in the organizational patterns of local government research across countries. A regularly updated register of specialized political science centres presenting their main characteristics and resources would be welcome and could be initiated by the IPSA research committee in the near future. For reasons of space limitation, it is not possible to list here in an exhaustive way these various modes of institutional settings. Yet three different portraits are briefly introduced below in order to mirror the structural diversity of research organizations. They are meant as illustrations of the varieties of infrastructure found in countries across the world.

CERVL, an illustration of the French tradition of strongly institutionalized research centres

Name:
CERVL – Pouvoir Action Publique Territoire
http://www.cervl.sciencespobordeaux.fr/eng_cervl%20accueil.htm
Affiliation:
The centre has two main institutional affiliations : CNRS (Centre National de la Recherche Scientifique/ National Center for Scientific Research), the largest public research organization in Europe – and Sciences Po Bordeaux, one of the main academic institutions devoted to political science in France, founded in 1948 with Maurice Duverger as its first director
Other significant CNRS teams in the field are:
In Grenoble : PACTE (Politiques Publiques, Actions Politiques, Territories: http://www.pacte.cnrs.fr/)
In Paris: CEVIPOF (Centre de Recherches Politiques de Sciences Po: http://www.cevipof.msh-paris.fr), CSO (Centre de sociologie des organisations: http://www.cso.edu/site/)
In Rennes: CRAPE (Centre de Recherches sur l'Action Politique en Europe: http://www.crape.univ-rennes1.fr/)

LGRU, an University based centre of excellence on British and comparative local government

Name:
Local Governance Research Unit, Leicester Business School, De Montfort University,
http://www.dmu.ac.uk/faculties/business_and_law/business/lgru_aboutus.jsp
Affiliation:
Its main affiliation is with the Department of Public Policy of Leicester Business School, at De Montfort University.
History:
This new centre of expertise in local government and politics opened its doors at De Montfort University, Leicester, in May 2004, under the direction of Lawrence Pratchett. LGRU focuses on research in key areas of local governance including public participation, political leadership and e-democracy.
Academic staff:
4 professors, 2 research fellows, 3 Ph.D students and post-docs.
Main orientations:
Local democracy and voting systems; public participation; local political leadership and management including executive models and scrutiny; e-demo-

cracy and voting options; local partnerships; and issues facing rural local authorities.
International cooperation:
The unit has strong research links with other universities in the UK and across Europe and the USA.

INLOGOV – Institute of Local Government Studies at the University of Birmingham

http://www.inlogov.bham.ac.uk/
The Department was founded in 1966 and employs 30 academic staff and 12 support staff. It produces three journals: Vista, Local Governance and Local Government Studies.
Current research fields include

- community governance
- political management
- leadership and management of change
- performance management and improvement.

Other research centres in the UK:

In Bristol: Cities Research Centre (http://www.built-environment.uwe.ac.uk/research/cities/)
In Birminghham: CURS (Center for Urban and Regional Studies: http://www.curs.bham.ac.uk/department/research.htm)
In London: The Greater London Group (http://www.lse.ac.uk/Depts/Greater/)
In Warwick: LGC (Local Government Centre: http://users.wbs.ac.uk/group/lgc/)

CLA reflects the recent emergence of local politics research centres in the South

Name:
Centre for Local Autonomy. 17-1, Hangdang-dong, Sungdong-ku, Seoul (South Korea).
http://fnf-cla.hanyang.ac.kr/english/eng_index.asp
Affiliation:
The CLA was jointly founded by the German Friedrich-Naumann Foundation and Hanyang University in Seoul. Hanyang University is one of the

leading private universities in Seoul, with a total of 20 various colleges and 12 postgraduate schools.

History:

An agreement was signed in 1986 between Hanyang University and the German Friedrich-Naumann Foundation regarding joint research projects. One year later the Centre for Local Autonomy was founded by both institutions. Its first director was Chang-hyun Cho (1987-1997), followed by Kee-Ok Rhee (1997-2001), and Eung-Kyuk Park (2001-).

Academic staff:

The Centre's current staff are 10 professors and 3 research assistants.

Main orientations:

The three main objectives of the CLA are:

1. Advancement of scholarship: to contribute to the advancement of scholarly research on local self government and democracy through historical, comparative, international and interdisciplinary approaches.
2. Advancement of local autonomy: to contribute to the advancement of Korean local autonomy through conducting surveys, research, training and consulting.
3. Advancement of international understanding and cooperation: to contribute to the development of understanding and cooperation between the Republic of Korea and Germany, through joint research, seminars and personnel exchanges.

Publications:

The Centre has published over 30 monographs and proceedings on various issues of local autonomy. Books contain the papers presented at the international and national seminars. Annually the "Local Administration Review" is published. A monthly bulletin has a circulation of more than 2000 copies, and is read by local government executives and council members, members of NGOs, scholars and researchers interested in local autonomy. Each bulletin contains analyses, commentaries and alternative policy recommendations on current issues of local autonomy authored by practitioners, scholars and journalists.

International cooperation:

Every year, scholars and practitioners from the U.S., Europe, Japan and other nations, join Korean specialists to conduct joint studies on significant issues of local autonomy from an international and comparative perspective. After the first seminar was organized in 1987 under the heading of 'Local Self-Government: A Comparative Approach', the 18th International Seminar on Local Autonomy was held in 2004 on "The Role of Local Governance in Transformation".

Other research centres

The Tokyo Institute of Municipal Research

http://www.timr.or.jp/eng/index.htm
TIMR was established in 1922 to study the urban policies of Tokyo and other cities (both in Japan and overseas) to achieve the following three major goals:

- improve urban governance;
- improve living conditions; and
- seek better solutions to urban problems.

TIMR has worked with governments and public and private research institutes in both comparative and collaborative studies.
The Institute has a research staff of 10 members and publishes a quarterly, Urban Affairs. The Institute's mission statement claims that, "Today, our challenges are to empower local governments in the midst of decentralization, and to seek solutions to increasing urban problems. TIMR is committed to respond to these challenges by conducting relevant and effective studies to help governments increase their capacity for good governance".

Moscow Carnegie Center

www.carnegie.ru
The Center has a regional program, which focuses on current analysis of various issues of Russia's regions, ranging from local elections to ethnic conflicts and the role of civil society in the regions. They also produce regular ratings of regional democratization in Russia. The head of the program is Nikolai Petrov (nikolay@carnegie.ru).

European University at St. Petersburg,Faculty of Political Science
and Sociology

http://www.eu.spb.ru/socio/index.htm
The faculty runs several research projects with an emphasis on Russia's regions, including studies of development of political parties in the regions, relationships between local governments and NGOs, reform of local government institutions in Russia's cities, and the impact of EU enlargement on political developments in Russia's North-West regions. The contact person is Vladimir Gel'man (gelman@eu.spb.ru)

The Institute of Sociology of the Academy of Sciences
of the Czech Republic

Established in 1990 as an independent institution principally engaged in the study of the Czech society and central social issues, the Institute is organised into 7 research groups, one of which focuses exclusively on changes in municipal and regional systems and social and cultural interaction across the Czech-German border. The institute publishes two journals, the *Czech Sociological Review* (in English) and *Sociologický casopis* (in Czech), as well as the bulletin *Data a fakta* (Data and Facts) and a number of working papers.

Center of Chinese Rural Studies

of Central China Normal University, Wuhan, Hubei
www.ccrs.org.cn/

Center for Public Administration, Zhongshan University, Guangzhou, Guangdong.

http://cpac.sysu.edu.cn/

Professional Associations

Some national political science associations have set up research committees on local/ urban politics/ government. These groups fulfil important functions for bridging and bringing together specialists in this area within a nation, although foreign participants are increasingly invited to join their activities. Usually they organize panels at annual or bi-annual national conferences, and/or set up special meetings on specific topics on an ad hoc basis. It also happens that research committees from several countries exchange information on a more or less systematic basis and decide to organize common meetings. The French and the German committees met together in this way at the University of Heidelberg in the Spring of 1996 at the initiative of their respective chairmen, Albert Mabileau and Hellmut Wollmann. Traditionally, a periodical newsletter was circulated among participant members, but the diffusion of Internet has frequently replaced this paper communication by more interactive and efficient means such as electronic newsletters and websites. In this way most of the information is easily updated and shared online within the respective communities of researchers: meetings, publications, prize announcements, jobs offers, data sources, etc.

The Urban Politics and Urban Policy Section of the American Political Science Association (APSA) has about 400 members. Its current President is

Hank Savitch (University of Louisville). Its website is available at the address: http://www.apsanet.org/~urban/, where regular information is provided on its activities. Dates and locations of future meetings on urban politics are also given, not only those of the APSA section but also of the Urban Affairs Association, Midwest Political Science Association, Southern Political Science Association, and Western Political Science. Within the APSA, a Comparative Urban Politics Group affiliated with the Urban Politics and Urban Policy Section has been set up in 2003. It organizes a short course during the annual meeting of the APSA for promoting comparative urban scholarship and research. The objectives of this training session are: to provide a framework for American urbanists to incorporate comparative perspectives into their existing courses on urban politics or to develop new courses on comparative urban politics; to consider how to undertake comparative urban research; and to bring together and organize people interested in comparative urban research.

The German Political Science Association (DVPW, Deutsche Vereinigung für Politische Wissenschaft) has a section on local politics, the Arbeitskreis LOPOFO (Lokale Politikforschung). It was created in 1972, chaired for a number of years by Hellmut Wollmann (Humboldt Universität Berlin), and now convened by Hubert Heinelt (Technische Universität Darmstadt) and Angelika Vetter (Universität Stuttgart). The LOPOFO website is available at the address: http://cms.ifs.tu-darmstadt.de/fileadmin/lopofo/ index.htm

The section organizes workshops at the annual meetings of the German Political Science Association Congress, and was responsible for the organization of the following meetings in the last years: "Institutions and Structures of Local Politics in the FRG", October 2004, Darmstadt; "Praxis without Theory? Scientific Discourses on the Distressed Neighbourhoods Programme - The Social City", May 2003, Stuttgart; "Reforming Local Government: Closing the Gap between Democracy and Efficiency", September 2002, Stuttgart; "Local Politics and Civil Society", Heppenheim, 2001.

The Local Politics Research Group of the French Association of Political Science (Association Française de Science Politique) was founded in 1994 by Albert Mabileau. It is currently chaired by Alain Faure (CERAT-CNRS/ Sciences Po Grenoble) and Jacques Caillosse (CERSA-CNRS/ University of Paris II). Its website is available at the following address: http://www.afsp. msh-paris.fr/activite/groupe/local/local.html. Several meetings were recently organized under its auspices, among them: 'Ideologies of territorial policies', CRAPE-CNRS, March 2004, Rennes; 'Decentralization of educational systems in Europe', MSH, October 2004, Paris; 'Local power and European policies', AFSP, January 2005, Paris.

Two specialist groups are organized within the British Political Studies Association: one on British and Comparative Territorial Politics, chaired by Jonathan Bradbury (University of Wales) and Nicola McEwen (University of

Edinburgh), and the other on Urban Politics, chaired by Josephine Kelly (Aston University).

International Academic Networks

Research
IPSA RC05 Comparative studies on local government and politics

The Research Committee on Comparative Studies on Local Government and Politics is one of the most long-standing committees of the International Political Science Association (IPSA). Founded in 1972, it has been successively chaired by Jerzy J. Wiatr (University of Warsaw 1972-1979), Francesco Kjellberg (University of Oslo, 1979-1985), Hellmut Wollmann (Humboldt University, Berlin 1985-1994), Harald Baldersheim (University of Oslo 1994-2003) and Vincent Hoffmann-Martinot (2003-). Its Secretary General is Norbert Kersting (Universität Marburg).

Its main objectives are:

- To develop local government research in political science, especially work based on international co-operation;
- To organize and maintain personal contacts among political scientists worldwide with an interest in local government and politics;
- To disseminate information and publish scholarly research;
- To provide a framework between individuals and organizations concerned with teaching and research in political and other social sciences.

Its new executive board elected in 2003 at the World Congress organized in Durban, South Africa, aims to facilitate exchanges between the different continents and to support initiatives from political science communities that are still not as dense and structured as in Europe or in North America.

In close cooperation with individual political scientists and local government research groups of national associations, the Research Committee supports international comparative meetings and research projects. Among its main objectives for the period 2004-2006 is helping to develop the International Metropolitan Observatory as well as projects analyzing transitional processes to local democracy and decentralized systems of governance.

It organizes a series of panels every three years at the IPSA World Congress; that last of these took place in Durban in 2003; the next sessions will be held in Fukuoka in Japan in 2006.

In addition to these regular meetings, the Committee sponsors international and regional meetings on various themes, the most recent of which are:

- 'Reforming local government: Closing the gap between democracy and efficiency', jointly organized with LOPOFO at the University of Stuttgart in September 2002.
- 'Hurst Seminar on Reform and Democracy in Local Government of Countries in Transformation', organized in May 2004 at the Ben Gurion University of the Negev, Beer Sheva, and co-sponsored by the IPSA Research Committee Politics & Public Policy.

The Committee's website is available at the following address: http://ipsa-rc5.sciencespobordeaux.fr/index.htm

ECPR Standing Group on Local Government and Politics

Convened by Bas Denters (Twente University, Institute of Decentralized Governance), LOGOPOL, the Standing Group on Local Government & Politics, is a well-established group of the European Consortium for Political Research that maintains an excellent electronic forum for highlighting current research, conferences, recent publications, and debates that might be of interest to specialists in the field.

The LOGOPOL is an essential tool for developing individual and collective research projects on local government and politics in Europe, in particular through the numerous and lively workshops and panels it sponsors each year at the ECPR Joint Sessions and every other year at the ECPR General Conference. It seems that no other similar regional political science structure exists in other regions of the world. It attracts also many non-European scientists, in particular from North America. Moreover, LOGOPOL is also involved in the organisation of the EUROLOC Summer School (see below).

Other networks

Three other international organizations deserve to be mentioned. They are not strictly political science institutions, but they actively contribute to interdisciplinary exchanges and initiatives in the area of local and urban studies. One of the first research committees created by the International Sociological Association was in 1969 the RC03 on Community Research. Chaired by Terry Nichols Clark (The University of Chicago), its activities are not only intense but also involve many social scientists from all over the world. Moreover, this committee has for over three decades maintained strong links with the IPSA RC05 so that communications flow almost daily between these two international networks.

Two other organizations have rapidly emerged in the last years as central platforms of connection and communication for political scientists specialized in urban politics and policies, the Urban Affairs Association, founded in 1969 under the name of Council of University Institutes for Urban Affairs (UAA; website: http://www.udel.edu/uaa/), and its sister organization, the European Urban Research Association (EURA: website: http://www.eura. org/), established in 1997. Both are clearly oriented towards interdisciplinary activities and offer unique opportunities to political scientists to work with urbanists, geographers, sociologists, and historians. Their annual meetings are attended by an increasing number of social scientists, mainly from America and Europe.

Training

The most innovative and enduring training initiative to our knowledge is the European Summer School in Local Government Studies, supported by the European Consortium for Political Research and its standing committee LOGOPOL. The purpose of the European Summer School in Local Government Studies is to bring students up-to-date on ongoing research, to inspire participants in relation to their own research, to create an atmosphere and surroundings which allow for a significant cultural, social and scientific exchange among students of different backgrounds, and to foster future cross-national working relations among the participants. The summer school lasts for ten days. The form alternates between lectures by professors, workshops where students present their own research papers, and workgroups where students discuss critical issues raised by the lecturers and present selected literature, as well as field trips to government institutions.

Responsibility for hosting the summer school alternates between 26 universities from 14 European countries (the EUROLOC-network). These 26 departments have engaged in a long-term cooperation with the purpose of developing specialized courses for Ph.D. students who follow formalized programmes in the field of local government studies or whose research and theses fall within that field. Concurrently with this activity, the network has during recent years carried out a major comparative research project on chief executive officers in European municipalities.[2]

Since the establishment of the network, seven Summer Schools have been held: in Odense (1995), Florence (1996), Oslo (1997) and Aabo (1999), Bordeaux (2000), Madrid (2001), Stuttgart (2002), Cork (2003), Twente (2004), and Budapest (2005) respectively. The work is coordinated by a com-

---

2   Books from the "U.Di.T.E. Leadership Study" include the following: *The Anonymous Leader: Appointed CEOs in Western Local Government.* Edited by Kurt Klaudi Klausen and Annick Magnier, Odense University Press, 1998; *Social Bonds to City Hall – How Appointed Managers Enter, Experience, and Leave their Jobs in Western Local Government.* Edited by Peter Dahler-Larsen. University Press of Southern Denmark, 2002; and *Leadership at the Apex: Politicians and Administrators in Western Local Governments.* Poul Erik Mouritzen and James H. Svara. University of Pittsburgh Press, 2002.

mittee with partly rotating membership. It is composed of the network coordinators – Poul Erik Mouritzen (Southern University of Denmark) and Lawrence Rose (University of Oslo) – the local organizer in the present year and the local organizer for the coming year.

The Nordic Local Politics Conference

is an annual event with objectives somewhat similar to that of EUROLOC, but limited to the Nordic countries, as the meetings are always conducted in the Nordic languages that are mutually understandable to the participants. Initiated in 1992 the meetings have been organised every year on a rotating basis among the core institutions although participation is open to all students and scholars with an interest in the field. The Conferences seek to combine the objectives of being a forum for training of doctoral students and a meeting place for scholars working in the field. These meetings held during the last weekend of November have become the major scholarly event in the field in the Nordic countries.

Information and Publication Resources

Libraries

It would be an impossible task to list all the libraries having large resources on local government and politics. The best advice to give to a beginner in this field looking for the few best locations in a given country would be to ask a highly competent specialized political scientist. It is pretty easy to identify in a country a couple of well equipped libraries. The choice is large in the US where academic libraries are mostly of a very high standard. In France, the best specialized libraries are to be found in the nine Institutes of Political Studies, in particular where the CNRS main research centres are hosted, in Paris (http://www.sciences-po.fr/), Bordeaux (http://www. Sciencespobor-deaux.fr/bibliotheques/), and Grenoble (http://www-sciences-po.upmf-grenoble.fr/rubrique44.html). But some other public libraries are essential, like those of the National Assembly (http://www.assemblee-nat.fr/) and the Senate (http://www.senat.fr/), or the site of French local authorities (http://www.carrefourlocal.org/). A quite impressive and systematic websites portal is offered in Germany under the name *Das Portal für kommunale Forschung und Praxis* (http://www.kommunalweb.de/).

The Internet revolution has made access to specialized documentation easier. You can now live in the pampas of Argentina and have, by clicking your mouse, direct access to works of the famous but geographically distant

Berlin specialist Hellmut Wollmann at the address: http://www2.hu-berlin.de/verwaltung/down.htm#hu. Individual researchers have begun to make their most recent productions available online, and this practice will surely continue to expand in the coming years. In addition to that a myriad of journals online are now offered by many academic libraries, through subscriptions to companies such as J-Store, Ebsco, Elsevier, and Muse.

Databases

Bibliographic databases greatly facilitate the fundamental stage of every research project, the review of literature. The most wide-ranging is IPSA-Abstracts, edited by Serge Hurtig (Fondation Nationale des Sciences Politiques in Paris) and Paul Godt (American University in Paris), available in a published form and in an electronic version (CD-ROM and by Internet). It is published bimonthly by the International Political Science Association under the auspices of the International Social Science Council, in co-operation with the International Committee for Social Science Information and Documentation and with the support of Unesco and the American University of Paris. Hundreds of journals of political science relevance are regularly analyzed and abstracted, including most of those of interest to specialists of local government and politics (see the 17 page long list of treated journals at the address: http://www.ipsa.ca/pdf/periodicals.pdf). In several countries, bibliographic databases on local affairs are also available like LOCALDOC (see above) in France and ORLIS in Germany (more than 270.000 references included since the 1970s at the address: http://www.difu.de/extranet/extranet-info/db-pro.phtml).

Obviously, the next step towards the digitalization of scientific information will be soon the generalized access to electronic books in political science. In 2004, the company Amazon launched a new free service in that direction: a new function, called *Search In the Book,* allows browsing and searching newly published books.

One of the most spectacular developments in social science infrastructure in the last twenty years has been the establishment of local databases that are systematically stored, documented, and easily available via Internet or other electronic means like FTP. These data are of various categories: census data, opinion surveys data, policy outputs data (for instance fiscal and budgetary measures).

The Inter University Consortium for Social Research (ICPSR)

The ICPSR has acquired a world wide reputation in collecting and making available hundreds of files vital for the social sciences community.

To give but one example, you can download from the University of Michigan website territorial data on Brazil collected in the 1940s-1960s by state. Here is the full corresponding description of these data:

Title: Aggregate Data Bank and Indices of Brazil, 1940-1960

Principal Investigator(s)

Schmitter, Philippe

Summary

This study contains data on the social, economic, and population characteristics of 22 states of Brazil in 1940, 1950, and 1960. For each of the three time periods, data are provided on the total population in urban and rural areas, industrial and commercial employment, and rural employment. Information is also provided on the literate population, eligible electorate, and actual voting electorate. The data ascertain the numbers of industrial and commercial establishments as well as membership in various unions, in art and literary associations, in sports organizations, in charitable organizations, and in Roman Catholic organizations.

Extent of Collection: 1 data file + machine-readable documentation (pdf)

Extent of processing: scan/ reform.doc

Data type: census data, and aggregate data

Time period: 1940-1960

Data source: Brazilian census publications

Data format: Card Image

Collection notes: The codebook is provided by ICPSR as a Portable Document Format (PDF) file. The PDF file format was developed by Adobe Systems Incorporated and can be accessed using PDF reader software, such as the Adobe Acrobat Reader. Information on how to obtain a copy of the Acrobat Reader is provided on the ICPSR Web site.

Sampling: The sampling frame consists of 22 states of Brazil in 1940, 1950, and 1960.

Bibliographic citation

Schmitter, Philippe. Aggregate Data Bank and Indices of Brazil: 1940-1960 [Computer file]. ICPSR version. Berkeley, CA: University of California, International Data Library and Reference Service [producer], 196?. Ann Arbor, MI: Inter-university Consortium for Political and Social Research [distributor], 1999.

Under the heading *Community and Urban Studies: Local Politics*, one can also access through the ICPSR website the data files of the following already classical research projects:

Citizen Attitude Survey: Urban Problems in Ten American Cities, 1970, National League of Cities. Urban Observatory Program.

Community Political Systems Study, 1962, Alford, Robert A., Scoble, Harry M.

Comparative Study of Community Decision-Making, Clark, Terry N.

Comparative Study of Community Power Research, 1920-1964, Gilbert, Claire W.

Impact of Urban Environments, 1966, Orbell, John

New Haven Community Study, 1959, Dahl, Robert A., and William Flanigan.

Quality of Life in the Detroit Metropolitan Area, 1975, Rodgers, Willard L., Robert W. Marans, et al.

San Francisco Bay Region Local Politics, 1966-1967, Eulau, Heinz, Prewitt, Kenneth

Survey of City Council Members in Large American Cities, 1982, Welch, Susan, Bledsoe, Timothy

United States Fiscal Austerity and Urban Innovation Project, 1983-1984, Clark, Terry Nichols, et al.

Urban Morality Issues Incidents in Ten Cities, 1990-2000: [United States], Sharp, Elaine B.

ADPSS – Archivio Dati e Programmi per le Scienze Sociali

(http://www.sociologia.unimib.it/sociodata/eng/home.htm) Adpss-Sociodata is a specialised unit in applying information methodologies to the analysis and archiving of research data in social sciences. It is the result of collaboration between the Istituto Superiore di Sociologia of Milan and the laboratory Sociodata, created in 1997 in the Sociological Department of Milan University (Faculty of Political Sciences). Adpss-Sociodata works inside the Department of Sociology and Social Research of the University of Milan - Bicocca in order to promote a "data culture", through the diffusion of hardware and software technologies, the creation of social sciences databases and the development of secondary analysis.

ASSDA – The Australian Social Science Data Archive

ASSDA (http://assda.anu.edu.au/) is located in the Research School of Social Sciences (RSSS) at The Australian National University (ANU). It was set up in 1981 with a brief to collect and preserve computer-readable data relating to social, political and economic affairs and to make the data available for further analysis. ASSDA collects data files from all parts of Australia, and from many different types of organisations, including universities, market research companies, and government organisations. Since its establishment, ASSDA has collected over 1050 datasets from Australian Surveys and opinion polls. ASSDA also holds Australian population Census data and data from other countries within the Asia Pacific region. The catalogue of holdings of ASSDA are available online.

CIDSP – Centre d'Informatisation des Données Socio-Politiques

(http://solcidsp.upmf-grenoble.fr/cidsp/index_gb.htm) is a CNRS funded social science data archive and research unit in collaboration with the University Pierre Mendès France and the Institute for Political Studies in Grenoble where it is located. Selected local politics data files: Local elections; Political communication in Isere; Fiscal Austerity and Urban Innovation in France; French women elected as mayors in 1989; Observatoire Interrégional du Politique surveys.

CIS – Centro de Investigaciones Sociològicas, Spain

(http://www.cis.es/home1024.aspx)
CIS conducts an average of forty studies per year, mostly surveys, but occasionally qualitative studies as well. CIS survey data are entered in the CIS Data Bank, where they are available to all citizens three months after information coding and processing is completed. In addition to nation-wide surveys, studies are conducted on social and political conditions in the different Autonomous Communities (i. e. regions) and major Spanish cities.

DDA – The Danish Data Archives

DDA is a national data bank for researchers and students in Denmark and abroad. The DDA is an independent unit within the group of Danish State Archives. This group consists of the Danish National Archives in Copenhagen, several Provincial Archives. Selected local politics data files include: Municipal Election Study, 1981; Working Conditions of Local Politicians, 1970-1974; Local Councils and Committees, 1978 and 1981; Members of Local Councils, 1995; The Municipal Organizations of Danish Politics, 2000; Local Politicians in Denmark, 1981-1982; Local Lists and Party Organizations, 1995; Local Elections in Denmark, 1909-1966; Local Organizations in Denmark, 1983; Municipal Administrative Departments and Management, 1980; Social Networks in Local Communities, 1985; Local Constituency Organizations in Denmark, 1982; European Municipal Chief Administrative Officers 1995, Denmark; Local Politicians and Local Elections, 1989; Danish Local Election Study, 1978.

ESDS – Economic and Social Data Service, UK

(http://www.esds.ac.uk)
The Economic and Social Data Service (ESDS) is a national data service that came into operation in January 2003. ESDS provides access and support for

an extensive range of key economic and social data, both quantitative and qualitative, spanning many disciplines and themes. It comprises a number of specialist data services that promote and encourage data usage in teaching and research. Examples of data files include: Public Attitudes Towards the European Parliament and Local Authority Elections (2004); Taste of Power: the Greater London Council (1980-86); Devolution and Decentralisation in Wales and Brittany (2001-02); Devolution and Constitutional Change (2001); Centre-Periphery Structures in Europe [1880-1978]: an International Social Science Council (ISSC) Workbook in Comparative Analysis; Politics and Spending in British Local Authorities (1949-67).

FSD – The Finnish Social Science Data Archive

(http://www.fsd.uta.fi/english/)
FSD is a national resource centre for social science research and teaching. It began operating in 1999 as a separate unit of the University of Tampere. FSD provides a wide range of services from data archiving to information services. Its primary goal is to increase the use of existing social science research data by disseminating it throughout Finland and also internationally. FSD is funded by the Ministry of Education. Selected local politics data files: City Service Survey 1983, 1985, 1989, 1997, 1993, 2001; Finnish Local Government 1992-2004; Finnish Local Government Barometer 1993-2000; Follow-up on Municipal and Europarliamentary Elections 1996; Municipal Environmental Administration Survey 1994, 1998; Networking of Welfare Providers 1994: Municipal Projects; Parties and Local Democracy 1996; Survey of Departing Local Councillors 1997.

GESIS – Central Archive for Empirical Social Research, Germany

(http://www.gesis.org/en/za/index.htm). The Central Archive collects primary material (data, questionnaires, code plans) and results of empirical studies in order to prepare them for secondary analyses and to make them available to the interested public. The range of the ZA encompasses all technical areas in which procedures of empirical and historical social research are used. Selected local politics data files: The Municipal Power Structure in a Commuter Municipality (1966); Merger Bonn-Bad Godesberg (1970); Municipality Study Juelich (Elite) (1971); Urban Development Data Collection (1969); Population and Municipal Re-Organization in the Cologne District (1972); Attitudes of Municipal Council Members from six West German Cities that are also Administrative Districts on Questions of Municipal Policy (1991-92); Cologne Study (1995); Cities and Municipalities (1990).

ISDC – The Israel Social Sciences Data Centre

http://isdc.huji.ac.il/
ISDC was established by the Faculty of Social Sciences at the Hebrew University of Jerusalem, with a mission to collect, preserve and distribute data of interest to the academic community. Since the early-nineties, it has become a national resource centre, disseminating data throughout Israel and, by arrangement with foreign archives, internationally. The ISDC now houses approximately 1000 datasets including national sample surveys, local studies, census micro-data and government records in selected fields as well as macro-economic and regional series. Several databases are available through the Web. Sources of data include the Central Bureau of Statistics (CBS), the National Institute of Insurance (NIOI), central and local government agencies, research institutes as well as independent researchers from affiliated institutes.

Norwegian Social Science Data Archive

(http://www.nsd.uib.no/english/)
The Commune Database contains statistics for all municipal units of administration in Norway since 1769. More than 190.000 variables are available on each unit, covering areas such as demographic and occupational information, electoral statistics, public economy and welfare state related statistics. The data base has detailed documentation on boundary changes, and provides coefficients for calculating estimated values when boundary changes occur. Included in the base are also coordinates that make it possible to produce thematic maps for any given set of units in the period from 1769 onwards. The Nordic Database on Regional Time Series contains county level information from censuses and elections in the five Nordic countries from 1950-1990. Vital statistics are available for the period 1945-1990. The data are organized in systematized time series. A system for computer mapping is also available.

SA – Steinmetz Archive, the Netherlands

(http://www.niwi.knaw.nl/en/maatschappijwetenschappen/steinmetzarchief/),
founded in 1962, is part of the Netherlands Institute of Scientific Information Services – NIWI of the Royal Netherlands Academy of Arts and Sciences – KNAW. The archive makes Dutch social science research data available to the public. Through the Steinmetz Archive, researchers in the Netherlands have also access to the collections of foreign data archives. Selected local politics data files: Citizen Surveys of the municipality of Heerlen 1993, 1995, 1997, 1998; Citizens of Eindhoven Survey 1996, 1997, 1999, 2000; City survey Venlo 1997; Civil participation in urbanisation report 1976; Appearance and

100

voting behaviour of migrants at municipal elections 1994; Decentralization and public assistance 1983; Decentralized government in Amsterdam 1981-1985; Dutch municipality council elections 1994, 1998; Local democracy and administrative renewal in seven Dutch municipalities 1991; Local leadership in the country-side 1969; Municipal police forces and retrenchment policy 1982; Municipal survey city of Ede 1993-97; Political interest in city of Tilburg 1966.

SADA – South African Data Archive

http://www.nrf.ac.za/sada/
The South African Data Archive (SADA) serves as a broker between a range of data providers (e.g. statistical agencies, government departments, opinion and market research companies and academic institutions) and the research community. It safeguards data sets and related documentation and attempts to make it as easily accessible as possible for research and educational purposes. Selected local politics data files: IDASA Political Culture Study (1997); IDASA Local Government Election Study (1995); Launching Democracy (1993-94); Migration and Settlement in the Cape Metropolitan Area (CMA) (1999).

SDA – Sociological Data Archives, the Czech Republic

(http://archiv.soc.cas.cz/enindex.phtml).
The Sociological Data Archive at the Institute of Sociology of the Academy of Sciences of the Czech Republic in Prague accesses, processes, documents and stores data files from sociological research projects and promotes their dissemination to make them widely available for secondary use in academic research and for educational purposes. Selected data files: Surveys of mayors, councillors, citizens 1991; surveys of mayors 1991; series of fiscal and demographic data on local communities.

SIDOS – Swiss information and data archive/service for the social sciences

(http://www.sidos.ch/index-e.html)
SIDOS is a foundation of the Swiss Academy of Humanities and Social Sciences (SAGW/ASSH). Established in 1992, SIDOS is the Swiss Data Archive for the Social Sciences. It maintains an inventory of social science research projects and data. Other domains include methodological validation and advice, as well as data retrieval. Selected local politics data files: Swiss local parties (1991); Political parties, administration and reforms in Swiss

municipalities – 1988, 1994, 1998; Survey of local chief administrative officers in Switzerland and their relationship to politics and parties (1988); Local power: between commune and Europe (1992); Size and local democracy (2002).

SSD – Swedish Social Science Data Archive

(http://www.ssd.gu.se/eng.html)
SSD is the national academic data service for Humanities and Social Sciences in Sweden, serving researchers at all Swedish universities with data for secondary analysis. Its main task is to preserve and disseminate quantitative and qualitative studies. The archive receives, processes and distributes data from researchers and research institutes at Swedish universities, Swedish public agencies and several Swedish private data producers. The Archive also receives and distributes the same kind of data from data archives world-wide. Selected local politics data files: Local elections 1966, 1970, 1979; Local citizen survey 1991; Greater Stockholm survey 1966; Local representatives 1968; Local politicians 1979-1980, 1993; Local government officers 1980; Local party organizations 1985, 1988; Functions of the press: Local councils and authorities; Local information activities 1979; Fiscal austerity and urban innovation; Sollentuna – A creative municipality; Opinion '90; Local government services – Determination factors and decision-making processes.

Book Series

Often series appears and disappears, so that only ongoing book series with an explicitly international social science and comparative focus are listed below.

Blackwell Publishing. Studies in Urban and Social Change

Series Editor(s): Margit Mayer, Harvey Molotch, Chris Pickvance, Linda McDowell
The Blackwell Studies in Urban and Social Change aim to advance debates and empirical analyses stimulated by changes in the fortunes of cities and regions across the world. Topics range from monographs on single places to large-scale comparisons across East and West, North and South. The series is explicitly interdisciplinary; the editors judge books by their contribution to intellectual solutions rather than according to disciplinary origin. This book series is linked to the journal, International Journal of Urban and Regional Research.

Ashgate – Urban And Regional Planning And Development Series

Series Editors: Peter Roberts and Graham Haughton
Incorporating a wide range of approaches to urban and regional studies, with an emphasis on original research linking theory and practice, this series is aimed at those working or studying in planning, geography, economics, sociology, public administration and political science.

The Ohio State University Press – Urban Life and Urban Landscape Series

Series Editors: Zane L. Miller
The series examines the history of urban life and the development of the urban landscape through works that place social, economic, and political issues in the intellectual and cultural context of their times. Specific areas of interest include the history of city planning; the history of neighbourhoods and communities; suburbs and suburbanization; landscape history and the history of urban design; the urban infrastructure; ethnic groups, blacks, and women in the city; and urban regionalism. Inquiries should be directed to Heather Lee Miller at The Ohio State University Press.

Sage – Cities and Planning Series

Sharpe – Cities and Contemporary Society
Series Editor: Richard D. Bingham
Today's cities present new challenges, offer new opportunities, and require new ways of looking at the urban experience. Books in the Cities and Con-temporary Society series are designed to chart a vision of urban life in the new millennium.

VS – Verlag für Sozialwissenschaften, Urban Research International Series

Series Editor(s): Hellmut Wollmann, Harald Baldersheim, Peter John
The volumes of the book series seek to provide a forum for the discussion of crucial issues of local and regional politics and government in an interna-tional and comparative perspective. The book series is edited in co-operation with the Research Committee on the Comparative Study of Local Politics and Government within the International Political Science Association.

Westview Press – Urban Policy Challenges

Series Editor(s): Terry Nichols Clark
Books in the Urban Policy Challenges series explore the range of urban policy problems and detail solutions that have been sought and implemented in cities from around the world. They build on studies of leadership, public management, organizational culture, community power, intergovernmental relations, public finance, citizen responsiveness, and related elements of urban public decision-making.

Journals

Most articles on local government and politics are published in national or regional journals of political science. Some are published in the official journal of the International Political Science Association the *International Political Science Review* (IPSR).
International Political Science Review
In April 1998, a special issue of IPSR (Vol. 19 Issue 2) was devoted to local and urban politics with the following contributions :
'Theory and urban politics', Gerry Stoker, p. 119, 11p.
'The making of citizenship in Argentinian local politics: between municipalization and municipalism', Mara Kolesas, p. 131, 16p.
'Sexing London: the gender mix of urban policy actors', Stefania Abrar, Joni Lovenduski, and Helen Margetts, p. 147, 25p.
'Urban politics in the 1990s: the difficult renewal of [North American] local democracy', Pierre Hamel, p. 173, 14p.
'Urban policy in ethnically polarized societies', Scott A. Bollens, p. 187, 29p.
'From local government to local governance – and beyond? Caroline Andrew and Michael Goldsmith, p. 201.
Other journals are specifically devoted to local or urban affairs, with an interdisciplinary orientation:

Community Development Journal

Editor: Chris Miller
Published four times a year and circulated in over 80 countries, the Community Development Journal provides an international forum for political, economic and social programmes, which link the activities of people with institutions and government. Dealing with the theory and practice of the policies, programmes and methods employed, the Community Development

Journal covers a wide range of topics including community action, village, town, and regional planning, community studies and rural development.

European Urban and Regional Studies

Editors: David Sadler, Ray Hudson, Allan Williams, and Gordon MacLeod
This journal provides a means of dialogue between different European traditions of intellectual enquiry on urban and regional development issues. In addition to exploring the ways in which space makes a difference to the future economic, social and political map of Europe, European Urban and Regional Studies highlights the connections between theoretical analysis and policy development. The journal also places changes in Europe in a broader global context.

German Journal of Urban Studies

Editors: Editors: Stephan Articus, Karl-Heinrich Hansmeyer, Helmut Klages, Heinrich Mäding, Christoph Reichard, Erika Spiegel, Klaus Stern, Christiane Thalgott
The German Journal of Urban Studies, like its predecessor of many years' standing, the Archiv für Kommunalwissenschaften, is a forum for all disciplines related to urban studies. The objective is to further the transfer of knowledge from research and scholarship to local government praxis, and of practitioners' experience and expectations to the academic community. The journal thus addresses scholars and researchers, all actors involved in local government-like councils, public authorities, industry, the media, and professional associations-and the interested (professional) public. The complete English language Internet version of the journal is found at http://www.difu.de/publikationen/dfk/en/.

International Journal of Urban and Regional Research

Editors: Alan Harding, Roger Keil and Jeremy Seekings
The International Journal of Urban and Regional Research (IJURR) is an international journal for urban studies. Since its inception in 1977 as a forum for intellectual debate, it has maintained a commitment to global and local issues and a cutting edge approach to linking theoretical development and empirical research. IJURR encompasses key material from a range of critical, comparative and geographic perspectives. Embracing a worldwide readership of over 50 countries and a multidisciplinary approach to the field, IJURR is concerned with the complex, changing roles of cities and regions.

Journal of Urban Affairs

Editors: Victoria Basolo and Rodolfo Torres
The Journal of Urban Affairs is a multidisciplinary journal devoted to articles that address contemporary urban issues and is directed toward an audience that includes practitioners, policy makers, scholars, and students. The Journal aspires to contribute to the body of substantive and methodological knowledge concerning public policies, programs, and administration. The Journal of Urban Affairs is the official journal of the international professional organization for urban scholars and practitioners, the Urban Affairs Association.

Kommunal Ekonomi Och Politik

Editors: Björn Brorström and Henry Bäck
"Kommunal Ekonomi och Politik" (Local Finances and Politics) is published in Scandinavian languages. The journal publishes, after peer-review, academic articles in the fields of local government politics and management. The journal is based in Sweden but has a circulation in all the Nordic countries to the academic community as well as to practitioners in local government. Among the authors scholars from all the Nordic countries are represented.

Local Government Studies

Editors: Colin Copus and Stephanie Snape
Local Government Studies is a leading journal for the study of the politics, administration and management of local affairs. The journal publishes articles which contribute to the better understanding and practice of local government and which are of interest to scholars, policy analysts, policymakers and practitioners. The focus of the journal is on the critical analysis of developments in local governance throughout the world. The editors particularly welcome studies of issues related to European local government. Local Government Studies provides a forum for the consideration of all issues related to sub-national levels of government.

State and Local Government Review

State and Local Government Review is published by the Carl Vinson Institute of Government of the University of Georgia and jointly sponsored by the Vinson Institute and the Section on Intergovernmental Administration and Management (SIAM) of the American Society for Public Administration. Since 1968, the Review has provided a forum for the exchange of ideas among practitioners and academics that contributes to the knowledge and practice of state and local government politics, policy, and management.

Urban Affairs Review

Editors: Susan E. Clarke, Gary L. Gaile, Michael A. Pagano.
Urban Affairs Review is a scholarly journal on urban issues and themes. It covers: urban policy, urban economic development, residential and community development, governance and service delivery, comparative/international urban research, social, spatial, and cultural dynamics.

Urban Studies

Editor: Ronan Paddison
Urban Studies seeks to provide an international forum for the discussion of issues in the fields of urban and regional analysis and planning. A hallmark of the journal is that it publishes articles from urban scholars working from within a variety of disciplines, including geography, economics, sociology and political science as well as planning and public administration.

Conclusion

We have tried to offer an overview of what the infrastructure of local government studies looks like in the contemporary political science community. Although this contribution can only reflect part of the reality, it traces main examples of research, training, information, and publishing developments that have taken place in the field at the national as well as at the international level.

A growth in the amount and variety of research means and institutions appears to be the most significant trend over the last thirty years. In addition to this quantitative trend, other important trends can be observed, such as the expansion of new scientific poles in continents where political science was for a long time rather weak like Africa and Asia, or developments towards a regionalization of scientific activities, in particular in Europe through the EUROLOC network or other collaborative efforts across national borders. Geographic and interdisciplinary mobility have considerably opened up the horizon of researchers involved in local government studies, so that the new generation of academics constitutes the key factor for enhancing the already firm movement towards more professionalization and internationalization of our field.

Chapter 5
An Assessment of the Field of Comparative Local Government Studies and a Future Research Agenda

Harald Baldersheim & Hellmut Wollmann

The purpose of this chapter is to develop a research agenda that reflects issues and concerns in the field of comparative local government studies as it enters the 21st century. To do this it is necessary to review concerns regarding the development of our object of study – local government around the world, as well as debates about the way we do research in this field. Do we as a community of scholars have the necessary theories and tools with which to address the issues that the actual evolutions or setbacks in local government entail? In some countries local government is of diminishing importance, in other places it is taking on new forms in response to new challenges, forms that deviate starkly from those we have previously known, while it seems to have difficulties taking roots in certain settings.

In the preceding chapters a foundation is laid for addressing these issues. Michael Goldsmith reminds us of the long and deep roots that support current research in the field; he also demonstrates that the research agenda has shifted in response to changing patterns of urban governance. New paradigms of research have emerged, indicating vitality and inventiveness of scholarship in the field. Recurring themes in research have been the nature of local power and the workings of institutions of democracy and their capacity to deliver policies demanded by various segments of the community. One of the issues that Goldsmith raises in particular is whether the classic local government institutions will be capable of delivering the goods in the larger, more complex and multi-cultural local communities that are emerging in cities around the world?

Susan Clarke takes this challenge further in outlining how scholars have sought to come to grips with the processes of globalisation and how these processes impact upon communities and local politics. Paradoxically, globalisation makes capital more footloose but also more sensitive to place. Footlooseness opens up spaces for local policy-makers trying to enhance the attractiveness of their communities but also heightens the competition between cities. Whether this narrows the range of policy options open to cities or stimulates innovation remains to be seen. Globalisation may intensify the problems of inclusion and inequality, and especially so the more cities acquire the character of "world city" – i. e. becoming preferred sites of global enterprises and decision-making. The latter may, however, happen at the cost of fragmentation of communities and governance.

Local government is a virtual laboratory for research. As pointed out by Peter John, the features of "numerosity" and "propinquity" offer advantages that drive theoretical development as well as relevance and realism in problem formulation. The great number of local authorities found in most countries, and certainly in cross-country surveys, allow for the use of advanced statistical techniques and generalisation of observations. At the same time, issues of local governance have a topicality that stimulates involvement and research that is rarely an ivory tower exercise. Involvement is not without its own problems, however, as highlighted in the last section of this chapter.

Since the 1970s the number of scholars involved in local government research has increased manifold and so have the institutions in which they work. As outlined by Vincent Hoffmann-Martinot, many countries have *Schwerpunkte* of research in this field, some of them more significant than others, perhaps. Data bases and document archives have been established that offer services to scholars both nationally and internationally. The latter feature, the international infrastructure for research, is perhaps a litmus test of the maturity of a field of research. Judged by this standard the study of local government has certainly come of age. Nevertheless, there are still challenges ahead with regard to enhancing international co-operation and cross-border efforts in this field of research. Addressing those challenges and opportunities is undoubtedly the road to further progress in the field.

But what are the issues that should serve as guidelines for further international and co-operative research? We shall search for further clues along two lines of inquiry: First, an assessment of developments and challenges to institutions of local government around the world, as presented in recently published reviews; this assessment is undertaken in particular with the aim of developing a research agenda that reflects the experiences of a wider selection of countries than has been covered in preceding chapters. Second, an evaluation of the field in the light of current epistemological debates in political science is undertaken.

The development of local government:
a review of issues and concerns

The preceding chapters outline a series of pressures on, and transformations of, established institutions of local government. The purpose of this section is to ascertain the extent to which transformation is actually taking place worldwide and to suggest how these transformations represent challenges to local government research. The countries reviewed below have been selected so as to represent the widest possible *contextual diversity* with regard to institution-building and/or institutional redesign. The contextual diversity extends from Western countries experimenting with New Public Management and competitive models of service provision, to post-communist states in transformation from one-party rule to local democracy, to Third World countries struggling with the legacy of colonialism and (in some cases) trying to reconcile village traditions with modern local government. What are the typical mechanisms of, and constraints on, change in these diverse contexts? What are the lessons for, and challenges to, research inherent in these change experiences? The latter issue will be addressed in particular in the last section of the chapter.

The institutions of local government: How adaptable?

In many *Western* countries (meaning, largely, OECD members), since the early 1990s, the emergence of the New Public Management (NPM) has been widely seen as the important challenge (or source of renewal, depending on one's point of view) to traditional local government, i. e. the multifunctional, politically "owned" service-providing organisation for and of the community. Consequently, a lot of research effort has been spent trying to ascertain the spread of the managerialist and market-oriented alternatives and their impacts (e.g. John 2001; Kersting and Vetter 2003; Denters and Rose 2005). This is not the place to go into details as to developments in individual countries or the more concrete details of NPM (Pollitt and Bouckhart 2004). Originating in the Anglo-Saxon world, particularly the UK in the Thatcher years and New Zealand and Australia, the perception of NPM has changed from that of a strategy for rolling back government into a source of ideas for more efficient government. As such it has crossed ideological divides and has also been adopted in deeply social-democratic countries such as Sweden and Finland. In its more managerialist version it was picked up by German local governments (*Neue Steuerungsmodel*); gradually, also, elements of competition are being introduced into the provision of local welfare services in Germany. The managerialist and market-oriented concepts have found less resonance in South European countries, however.

The NPM-oriented reforms have had the most dramatic impact in the UK, where local government remains only a shadow of its former self. Local government has been shorn of functions and put under a national regime that has severely curtailed spending and taxation powers. A number of independent bodies have been set up to perform educational and developmental functions that used to be the task of local authorities. Inspectorates and complaints procedures have sought to empower the customer-citizens, with the help of the state and the power of competition (Sullivan 2003). As a

111

result, the structure of local government has become highly fragmented. The New Labour government has revised only a few of the measures introduced by the former regime (such as compulsory, competitive tendering and value-for-money-driven service provision); local government remains fragmented despite talk about the need for more "joined-up government", so much so that British scholars have coined a new term to capture the disjointed local scene: *local governance*, referring to the need or capacity to organise collective action through the voluntary pooling of resources across disconnected institutions (Stoker 2004), a job that used to be done through integrated local authorities. In most other countries, however, NPM has resulted in more limited modifications of local government institutions and operations (Kersting and Vetter 2003)[1].

The heated debate on the merits of NPM has somewhat overshadowed other reform initiatives taken by local governments, such as policies for *democratic inclusion* and enhancement of *transparency and political accountability* (Kersting and Vetter 2003; Denters and Rose 2005). Strategies for democratic inclusion cover such measures as neighbourhood councils, popular initiatives, local referenda, etc. Experiments with neighbourhood government date back at least to the 1970s and the famous Bologna model, which spread to a number of other countries, reaching a peak in the 1980s but still a significant force in a number of cities around the world (Bäck et al. 2005). Popular initiatives refer to measures to empower citizens to bring issues directly on the agenda of local councils; such initiatives usually require a certain number of citizen signatures to oblige the council to consider the issues. Countries that have passed such citizens powers into the national legislation include Norway, Finland, France, Germany, Croatia, and Portugal among others. Holding local referenda is now permitted in most European countries (Council of Europe 2000); only a few have opened up for binding referenda, however (mostly the new German *Länder* and some post-communist countries).

A number of countries have also been concerned with transparency and accountability in local politics. Introducing *directly elected executives* as a clear focus of responsibility has becoming a widespread strategy for enhancing accountability. Until the 1990s, directly elected mayors were largely confined to a number of American cities under the strong mayor model and to two South German *Länder* (Bayern and Baden-Württemberg). During the 1990s direct elections have been adopted in the other German *Länder* as well as by a number of post-communist countries and South European countries

---

1   Denters and Rose (2005) suggest the occurrence of somewhat more far-reaching changes, especially with regard to the introduction of NPM measures; they also caution readers, however, as to the actual extent of change with the provisos that, "the same label may be used for widely different practices; and... new features are at times more symbolic than genuine in character" (p. 261).

such as Portugal, Greece and Italy. In the UK the choice of direct elections is optional while some Norwegian municipalities have been permitted to hold direct mayoral elections on an experimental basis. This trend could be seen as the spread of a new type of local political system – from government through committees to presidential systems of government.

In the United States, with its great variation of local government systems, debates on advantages and disadvantages of specific institutional choices are of long standing. The overall pattern of local government may appear fragmented (Savitch and Vogel 2005). However, in terms of executive organisation there are still two prevailing patterns: the mayor-council model and the council-manager or corporate model. The merits of "reformed" (council-manager) and "unreformed" (mayor-council) systems respectively have engaged decision-makers as well as scholars (cf. Banfield and Wilson 1963 for a review of the debate). According to Savitch and Vogel, "In the last decade, major trends in local government management include (1) an emphasis on executive-centred governance, and (2) efforts to fashion public-private partnerships" (Savitch and Vogel 2005: 213).

Another issue of long standing in the American debate on urban governance is that of finding structures for co-ordinating fragmented metropolitan areas. This is an issue that increasingly finds an echo among reformers around the world, as urban areas expand beyond the traditional boundaries of a central city. The classical solutions to the problem, amalgamation or a two-tier system, have both proved hard to achieve, often because of resistance from suburban authorities. In this respect, North America displays an interesting contrast between the US and Canada (Sancton 2002). During the 1990s the Canadians launched a series of initiatives to introduce overarching metropolitan governmental structures for major urban areas (Halifax, Toronto) that were not already covered by such institutions (like Calgary). These are now in operation. The Canadians seem more willing to accept overarching governmental structures for their urban areas, whereas Americans prefer the more fragmented structures. The discrepancy may have more to do with contrasts in class and race composition between Canadian and American cities than a greater acceptance of rational choice prescriptions regarding the virtuous of fragmented structures in the American case (Sancton 2002: 188).

The developments outlined above indicate that there have certainly been reforms in Western local government, these have largely meant *institutional modifications* of existing patterns (with the exception of the radical British changes). The path dependency of institutional choices (i.e. the constraints engendered by previous choices) and the institutional staying power predicted by neo-institutional theory (Peters 1999) seem vindicated by the reform history of Western countries. No convincing argument has been put forward to account for the British *Sonderweg* – a development that is the more surprising since Britain has often been hailed as the most tradition-bound of countries.

Japan is also a case of institutional modification. NPM has made only marginal inroads in Japanese local government. During the latter half of the 1990s, retrenchment of the national economy and pressure from an aging population induced individual local authorities to pick up new management practices. One of the innovative local governments was the Mie Prefecture (in Japan, the 47 prefectures are counted as local governments). The prefecture's policy evaluation scheme, for example, has been emulated by a number of cities (Nakamura 2002: 178). Measures such as benchmarking (comparison of performance), performance-related pay and outsourcing are also spreading gradually. The most important reforms of the 1990s, however, were legislation enhancing local autonomy. Hundreds of laws were changed or abolished, while new enabling legislation was enacted (1995). National controls over local decision-making were reduced. Services were transformed from state to local functions, expanding the scope of local responsibilities so that a new model of central-local relations came into operation from April 1, 2000 (Nakamura 2002: 174).

The post-communist countries demonstrate a quite different scenario. Here it is appropriate to talk about an *institutional revolution* set in motion by the political earthquake triggered by the collapse of the communist regimes. Establishing institutions for local democracy was among the early reforms introduced by the new elites that emerged in East-Central Europe in 1989 (for a review of post-communist local reforms, cf. Baldersheim et al. 2003). The new institutions, built on the standards of democratic local government as outlined by the Charter of the Standing Conference on Local Government of the Council of Europe, broke radically with the dominant model of welfare provision under the communist regimes. The communist welfare model was centred on the workplace and the large combinat, which offered kindergartens, education, medical services, pensions, holidays and everything else for the workforce. The combinat was a welfare agency just as much as a place of work. The change from government through the workplace to government through and for the community was a true revolution. The formal establishment of the new institutions was swift, filling them with realities took longer, and, naturally, the process was not painless nor an even one. Nevertheless, the essential features of democratic local government were put in place in less than one year in the East-Central European countries; local elections were held, an administrative apparatus was established, and functions were carried out. The institutional choices were not carbon-copies of one particular model; Poland, Slovakia or Hungary devised institutional solutions with distinctively national flavours, so that it is not possible to talk about one particular post-communist model of local government. In this sense there was no pronounced post-communist path dependency. It would be more correct to say that these countries broke away from the communist path.

However, three weak points emerged in the ensuing structure of local government of the East-Central European countries: the financial foundation was weak, so that local government was mostly financed by transfers from central government. And the range of functions was limited – central government was slow to transfer functions to the local level. Both of these weaknesses reflected communist legacies. In many communities the old combinats could not manage the switch to a market economy and disappeared, while unemployment rose. Consequently, there was little wealth and income at the local level from which to generate revenues. Furthermore, property relations remained tangled for a long time, so that property taxes were difficult to introduce. The reluctance to decentralise more functions could partly be explained by the small scale of many of the new municipalities. In several countries, in the somewhat anarchic situation of transition, many communities took the opportunity to undo previous amalgamations and establish more small-scale local government on a village basis. Especially Czechoslovakia and Hungary emerged rather territorially fragmented, Hungary with over 4000 municipalities, for example, and Slovakia with more than 6000. The third weakness was the problem of the *meso* level or the difficulties in agreeing on regional subdivisions, which meant that viable *meso* government was only established shortly ahead of EU accession of 2004.

In what may be called the core area of previous communist dominance, *Russia and the former Soviet republics*, the difficulties of democratic transition at the local level were even more pronounced. Russia was a case of many starts and stops, of contradictory initiatives, half-hearted decentralisation and reversals of legislation. In 1990, as part of Gorbachev's reforms, legislation was introduced establishing local government that corresponded largely to the standards of the Council of Europe. The local elections in March 1990 were a turning point in establishing local councils with a local mandate independent of higher authorities and *nomenklatura* practices (Wollmann and Butusova 2003: 214). Subsequent power struggles at the national level resulted in a gradual subordination of the local structures to national power figures, first Yeltsin, later Putin, through a curtailing of functions and national appointment of the local executives. Thus, Russian local government has been described as being in a precarious situation between "the rule of law" and "the logic of power" (Wollmann and Butusova 2003).

It should be pointed out, however, that in other parts of the former Soviet empire, local government is taking root, for example in the Baltic countries, and seems to be functioning reasonably well (Vanags and Vilka 2003).

How can this complex pattern of institution-building in the post-communist area be accounted for? – An early, widespread and enthusiastic acceptance of the standard model of local self-government (LSG) in all of the countries, a somewhat tortuous and lengthy period of implementation in most of the countries, and a series of half-starts and reversals in some of the countries? The interaction of three logics may illuminate these developments. The first logic is that of *politics of identity*. The ideological reorientation that could be expressed openly from 1989 was one of kinship with Western Europe, its economic and political systems. Intellectual elites in Czechoslovakia and Hungary had already in the 1980s sought to carve out a special place for their countries by insisting on being part of "Central Europe", as distinct from "Eastern Europe", distancing themselves from what they saw as an Asiatic heritage of the more Eastern parts of the continent (and by implication the Soviet Union) (Kundera 1984; Schöpflin and Woods 1989). The enthusiasm for European standard local government was part of a wider reconstruction of identities in the image of Western liberal traditions. Second, the actual implementation of those institutions were hampered by a multitude of *practical limitations* (financial, legal, lack of expertise, etc) so it was small wonder that the implementation and early operation would have something of a learning by trial and error character. Third, the stop-start and reversal processes that Russia illustrates so well have been largely driven by the logic of *national power struggles*, in which control over the local scene was part of the stakes. Additionally, the attraction of Western identities may have exerted a weaker pull in the Russian case – Russian elites were always divided in their identities, between those with inclinations towards Western traditions and those that saw Russia's destiny in more Slavic terms (Seton-Watson 1984/1989).

In many *Third World countries* establishing institutions of democratic local government has encountered serious barriers. The history of local government is often one of reversals or inertia. Reviewing post-colonial experiences in local governance in sub-saharan Africa, a Nigerian analyst writes that "Unfortunately, the experiment to develop modern local institutions in Africa has been fraught more with failures than successes" (Olowu 1995: 1). The problems in making local institutions work were partly those of reconciling traditional community structures of governance (chiefdoms) with modern national institutions, and partly those of centralised national strategies of development that left little room for local self-government. The latter obstacle was of course compounded by the spread of the one-party state in so many African countries.

Since the early 1990s decentralisation reforms have been under way in most countries of the African continent. Perhaps the most insistent steps have been taken by South Africa with its decentralisation programme of 1998, which involved large-scale amalgamations in order to extend municipal services to black townships and rural areas that were previously grossly neglected by existing service provisions. The elections of 2000 established a series of larger municipalities and district authorities with the aim of overcoming the legacies created by a history of racial segregation. The primary function of the new local authorities was seen as that of driving economic and community development. To achieve this municipalities are to draw up so-called "integrated development plans" with an emphasis on participatory mechanisms; the participatory element seems somewhat unevenly achieved (Cameron 2005). However, the job is not an easy one, as Tom Lodge observes, "For South Africa's new rulers, the creation of accountable municipal administration has constituted one of the most difficult challenges they have encountered. Even in larger towns, in which the ANC could draw upon deeper layers of competent leadership and richer material resources, the first five years of democratic local authority has been a chastening experience" (Lodge 2002: 99). The performance of the new institutions may depend among other things on "more equitable resource allocation and tougher ethical standards .... among officers than prevail at present" (Lodge 2002: 128). Some of the problems of local government may also be accounted for by a discrepancy between the stringency of the central government's macro-economic policies and the redistributionist aims of local development plans (Cameron 2005).

A recent review of local democracy and politics in South Asia was subtitled *Towards internal decolonization?* (Vajpeyi 2003). The authors argue that institution-building in these countries (India, Pakistan, Bangladesh, Nepal, Sri Lanka) had to grapple with a legacy of colonialism, which has shaped responses to local democracy. The new national elites took over not only many of the institutions left by the old colonial masters (the British) but also their condescending attitudes to the "natives" – the ordinary people. While the British legacy of a national civil service made for fairly efficient administration of national functions, there were no democratic local institutions. These were either created from scratch or sought to combine traditional village level rule of elders with elements of modern institutions. In India, it took until 1959 for the first nation-wide legislation for local government to be passed. A three-tier system was introduced opening up for grass-roots participation at the local level. The system was short-lived, however, and faded away after Nehru's death (Vajpeyi and Arnold 2002: 39). Constitutional amendments of 1992 introduced a new system, guaranteeing the status of local bodies and restricting the states' powers of intervention. The fiscal foundations of local governments remain extremely weak and uncertain, however.

The history of local government in Bangladesh is one of constant reshuffles under changing regimes (whether military juntas or elected governments) to serve the ends of the powers of the day. Local elections have only been held intermittently and have been of little consequence for local policy-making. Constitutional requirements regarding the establishment of LGS were not implemented until 1976, and then only half-heartedly. The military government of general Ershad introduced a system of directly elected councils supplemented with *ex officio* members charged with drawing up development plans for their respective regions. These bodies were largely dominated by the rural elites (Khan and Obaidullah 2002: 77). The return to democratic rule in 1991 was accompanied by shifting recommendations for new local government structures, the latest of which suggested establishing a four-tier structure from the village to the district level. Summing up their observations Khan and Obaidullah write that "the local government system (LGS) – both rural and urban – remains beset with problems. Politically, financially and administratively the LGS continues to depend heavily on central government and hence all its activities are significantly moulded by the latter. The colonial legacy of a dependent and subservient LG continues unabated" (Khan and Obaidullah 2003: 88-89).

Sri Lanka has had a system of democratic local government since independence. This was at first a continuation of the municipal and urban councils introduced during British rule (Oberst 2002: 126). Since independence these were elected bodies. Over time the structure has been consolidated into a smaller number of municipal, urban and rural councils. Turnout at local elections is high (70 pct. or more). The actual operations of the system suffer from two major weaknesses: First, a narrow revenue base (no separate base) and consequently little money available for local councils; second, the current debate on decentralisation is heavily influenced by the state of civil war on the island, making it extremely difficult to reach compromises on the further extension of functions to local government. Local councils are, therefore, "... primarily local honor societies that provide the prestige of membership to their members and some patronage benefits" (Oberst 2002: 127).

In Pakistan, the political instability at the national level has left local government largely as responsibility of the provincial governments with guidance from various ordinances of the central government; there are no constitutional provisions for local self-government. A Devolution of Power Plan introduced in 2000 envisaged a new three-tier structure with extended powers for the new councils at the various levels. The voting age was to be lowered to 18 years; special provisions were made for female representation (one third of seats reserved for women). It remains to be seen whether the proposed reforms will change the traditional situation in which "Local government controlled and administered by provincially appointed bureaucrats has been the long-accepted model in Pakistan" (Vajpeyi 2002: 146).

This brief review of efforts at democratising local government institutions in sub-Saharan and South Asian countries does not, of course, exhaust the list of 3rd world experiences[2] (for example, Porto Allegre's experiment in

---

2   China's attempts at decentralisation in recent decades are not included in this review for the simple reason that these steps towards greater flexibility in local decision-making cannot be considered as democratic initiatives; China remains an authoritarian one-party state with party officials in dominant positions at all levels of governance (cf. Caulfield 2005 for a review of China's decentralisation reforms).

Participatory Budgeting is spreading to communities world wide (Harris et al. 2004). We do think, however, that the examples are fairly typical of developments in many Southern countries[3]. The hypothesis to be extracted from these examples is that there may be certain preconditions that have to be met for democratic local government to take root. One of these may be political stability at the national level; if national elites cannot agree on the institutional choice for local government, and successive regimes repeal whatever has been established by their predecessors, then, naturally, local democracy will be stunted. Russia also illustrates this precondition. A second precondition suggested by these examples pertains to the local context: if the communities into which institutions of local democracy are being introduced are permeated by stark inequalities in terms of class, caste or property, the weaker groups will have difficulties in asserting their interests; this is illustrated by all the South Asian countries reviewed above. A third precondition concerns culture and identity. While it may be difficult to describe precisely the cultural pre-requisites of democracy (cf. Almond and Verba 1963 for a suggestion), culturally ingrained notions of the role of women, for example, influence conspicuously the local democratic processes in this part of the world (cf. the legally prescribed female quotas on local councils, for example, to counteract the impact of such notions); furthermore, widespread attitudes to positions of authority seem to give civil servants an upper hand in dealings with local councils (Jamil 1999), restricting the reach of real decentralisation.

The policies of local government: how diverse and innovative?

Historically, the functions of local government have been of a technical and mundane nature. The core functions have been local infrastructure and sanitation such as sewers, roads, street lighting, garbage collection, sometimes also public health and police functions. Modern local government emerged as a response to the problems and requirements of industrialisation and urbanisation. In some countries, especially in Northern Europe, the functional palette has expanded into that of a mini-welfare state, in other countries it has remained limited to the core functions. With the politicization of local government came an interest in understanding its consequences in terms of *policy choices*. Local policy choices have been on the research agenda of students of local government just as long as those of institutional choices. The 1960s saw a surge of interest in understanding variations in policy choices across jurisdictions, culminating in controversies over the question "Does politics matter?" (cf. Boyne 1985, 1996 for a review).

---

3 Harris et al. 2004 when applying the more exacting criteria of *substantive* and *participatory* democracy in their analysis of local democratisation of the Philippines, Indonesia, Kerala, South Africa and Brazil demonstrate that by such standards, local democracy may seem even more difficult to achieve than indicated by the review above.

A parallel research focus asked questions about the origins of and pre-conditions for *policy innovation*, especially regarding policies of relevance for decaying inner cities. The interest in policy innovation was the driving force in the international project Fiscal Austerity and Urban Innovation, in which the fiscal retrenchment that hit local government in many countries during the 1970s and early 1980s was expected to stimulate new policy responses. Retrenchment was even expected to give birth to a new political culture characterised by unorthodox fiscal policies (combining preferences for low taxes and expansive welfare policies!) (Clark and Ferguson 1983). British research recognised that policy preferences and expertise could be a uniting force across levels of government, shaping *policy communities* that serve to set policy standards across formally independent local jurisdictions (Rhodes 1997), reducing the variations that might otherwise be expected to arise from contrasts in party constellations and other local conditions.

Others have seen the reduction of potential policy variation as an inherent feature of the economic environment in which local government operates in capitalist society. Paul Peterson (1980) argued that the absence of redistributive urban policies was a natural response of municipalities that have to compete with each other for private investments. Redistributive policies with their concomitantly higher taxes would drive away potential investors and jobs and would therefore be shunned by working class voters as well as their employers. Marxist analysts have tried to relate the tasks of municipalities to the more general division of work in capitalist society, with cities given the role of bridging the fundamental conflicts inherent in a capitalist economy (i.e. by taking on the functionally necessary role of regenerating labour that would otherwise be mercilessly and self-defeatingly exploited into the ground by competing fractions of capital).

The growth machine thesis gave cities a somewhat more creative role, in which they could pursue policies of urban and economic regeneration, stimulating urban development, although with investors and businessmen in the driving seat or at least with their interests uppermost in the mind of decision-makers (Logan and Moltoch 1987).

Towards the end of the 1980s the positions outlined above seemed increasingly incapable of accounting for the actual variation on local policies, as cities became more concerned with destandardising policies and service provision. Scholars began pointing out parallels between trends in local service provision and the more flexible patterns of production in industry that was gaining ground first in Japan and then spreading to other countries. Tailor-made production and just-in-time delivery were seen as expressions of a new economic order – post-Fordism, driven by the more rapidly shifting demands of customers (Stoker 1990). The argument of the French regulation theory school was that mass production was coming to an end in industry, and work practices were following suit. Similar trends were under way in public administration, signalling the fall of machine bureaucracy and standardised service provision. To many municipalities, NMP was the institutional answer,while more adaptive service provision was the policy response.

Towards the late 1990s *local policy responses to a changing environment* became the central focus in research and debate. Globalisation, ICT, multi-culturalism, poverty, alienation (from apathy to its most threatening form, terrorism) are some of the factors seen as driving urban policies (or requiring policy responses, when they are not forthcoming). Scholars have made considerable efforts trying to map these policies and develop theories to make sense of them, as outlined by Susan Clarke in chapter 2. Despite these efforts we are still able to understand only vaguely the contours of the new world, what the role of local government may be in this world, and what sort of policies that may be adequate responses.

Is local government headed anywhere? Convergence or divergence? Change or inertia?

Two somewhat contradictory impressions emerge from the reviews of local government developments in this and the preceding chapters: On the one hand, accounts are given of tremendous changes being imposed upon local governments and their populations, driven by the forces of globalisation; local authorities are struggling to adapt their structures, procedures and policies to keep up in the global race. The post-communist revolutions represent another story of sweeping change, brought about by internal collapse as well as external pressure. On the other hand, the reports coming from many other countries are ones of stability if not down-right inertia in local government institutions; even where far-reaching change is sought, e.g. in South Africa or India, results have been disappointing. South Asian scholars speak of the persistence of "internal colonialism". Even New Public Management enthusiasts have introduced no more than marginal change in most places. By these accounts, local government institutions seem extremely path dependent. While the first set of analyses paints a picture of local change driven largely by external factors, i.e. globalisation, the second set describes local institutions that are almost held prisoners by their own pasts and their local contexts. How are such seemingly contradictory trends to be analysed? This is the issue to which we turn in the next section.

Problem- or theory-driven research?

In a recent volume on "problems and methods in the study of politics" (Shapiro et al. 2004) the discipline of political science is portrayed as a battlefield of warring camps in pursuit of highly disparate agendas worshipping conflicting ideals of scientific endeavour. The overarching front line of the discipline is identified as that between advocates of *problem-driven* research versus champions of *methods- and theory-driven* studies. The former are seen as seeking to focus their research on important real-world problems and choosing methods and theoretical departures eclectically as demanded by the problems at hand. The relevance of research is an overarching value.

Those presented as giving primacy to methodological and theoretical concerns prioritise above all analytical rigour and explanatory elegance in their work, aiming for cumulative research and, at the end of the day, unified science. The argument levelled against problem-driven research as a scholarly ideal is that while there is nothing wrong *per se* with addressing important real-world problems in political research, the danger with this as an overarching strategy is that research risks never becoming much more than (hopefully) well-informed journalism (Shapiro et al. 2004: 2). The accusation against method-driven research is that of sterility of analysis, lack of realism in assumptions and narrowness in range of issues brought under study ("looking under lamp posts for the key"). The underlying schism is claimed to be one between adherents of some version of rational choice theory, striving to develop simplifying (or what they themselves would call parsimonious) models of political processes, and scholars of other persuasions who feel that understanding is best promoted through strategies of immersion into their field of study through "thick description", narrative or (de) constructivist strategies, or simply old-fashioned case studies. "Scientific" versus "interpretive" scholarly perspectives are one set of labels applied to these positions (Hoeber Rudolph et al. 2004: 386). In a summing-up statement of his own view Robert Dahl argues that the complexity and contingency of political processes necessitate a division of labour with regard to how research is carried out; methodological orthodoxy as well as a goal of unified science are undesirable objectives; and seeking *to help achieve good ends* is the best justification of a political science (Dahl et al. 2004: 378-381).

Dahl's position rhymes well with the historical development of the social sciences in general, not only that of political science. Economics, sociology and political science grew out of practical issues faced by administrators and policy-makers as the modern state came into being during the 18th and 19th centuries (Wollmann 2005); subsequently, the expansion of the welfare state drove demand for research on policy issues raised by ambitious post-war programmes, stimulating the development of new theories and research techniques. Harold Lasswell's famous programme for *policy sciences* was an attempt to formulate a research orientation that was both scientifically sound and of practical relevance in such a context (Lasswell 1951).

As regards the choice of theoretical models and methods of research to grapple with the research agenda at hand, the subfield of local government studies is probably as heterogeneous as any other subfield of political science. It is not difficult to point to numerous examples of rational choice type of analysis, for example; nor is there any lack of surveys and use of statistical techniques; case studies have a strong position while narrative approaches have been applied especially to tap the experiences of out-groups in cities, etc. In fact, studies of local politics have been somewhat of a laboratory for the development of research methods (cf. for example the debates engendered by the community power studies, as outlined in chapter 1, or the review of methodological approaches in chapter 3).

From the previous chapters and also from our own experience we think it can also be safely concluded that a large proportion of studies in the field of local government and politics share the characteristics of *problem-driven* research. This may even be stated as one of the hallmarks of research in the field, to be added to those of numerosity and propinquity suggested by Peter John (chapter 3). Students of local government have almost programmatically sought out the problems in urban development and institutions of local government as their subjects of research. They have frequently been involved in research programmes initiated by governments hoping to find answers to pressing issues of the day. Their research has added insights although it may not always have been fully heeded by the government that asked for illumination in the first place.

Frequently, the studies undertaken have been in the format of *evaluation* research, which is not only problem-driven but also characteristically committed to providing *advice and recommendation* for reformers. Initiated in the US in the late 1940s, think tanks and contractual research are now world wide phenomena (Wollmann 2003). An early example that comes to mind is the research on the urban initiatives under the War on Poverty programme in the United States of the 1960s. Later examples include the evaluation programmes of the Scandinavian Free Commune Experiments and the studies on the French decentralisation wave under the Mitterrand presidency, or the British research programme on the Thatcher legacy and the New Labour revisions conducted in the 1990s. The post-communist local democracy projects have also been subjected to numerous evaluation studies.

However, we doubt that research in the subfield of local government and politics studies can be easily *divided* into problem- versus theory-driven research. Rather, much of the research is *both* problem- and theory-driven, i. e. *research that aims at testing theories on data that reflect practical problems and issues of the day or is motivated by a desire to develop theories that can make sense of current challenges.* Evaluation research seeks to ascertain and assess the impacts of or preconditions for public interventions through institutional or policy choices. Such an ambition always necessitates the construction of an explanatory model of some kind (even when the model is one that emphasises *understanding* rather than identification of causal factors). This means that theoretical ambitions are inherent in the research effort. In our view, this particular feature of the subfield constitutes *an alternative way* between problem- and theory-driven research. We shall return to an outline this of direction in the concluding section of the chapter and shall also provide an assessment of its relevance with regard to understanding the emerging challenges to local government and politics – so far as such challenges may be discernible at present.

Conclusions: the study of local government and politics as the laboratory of the policy sciences

It is our conviction that progress in research will be made if we as a scholarly community can preserve some of the best features of the community while at the same time paying attention to the challenges that have emerged from the preceding chapters and assessments. First of all, *the combination of problem- and theory-orientation* should be maintained and its virtues more highlighted. The very subject matter of the field – local government and politics – ensures that the problems of research are also problems of the day, of immediate relevance to the daily lives of most citizens. Propinquity makes for relevance and realism in problem formulation. The other essential feature of the subject matter – numbers and variation of local authorities – means that local government is a vast laboratory, a testing ground for theories of institutional development and political and economic behaviour. In terms of scholarly orientation we advocate a (re-) connection to the Lasswellian tradition in making use of the unique research opportunities presented by the vast range of municipal institutions and policies. As regards an epistemic foundation the *realist scientificism* proposed by Imre Lakatos (1970) seeks to fuse elements from positivism as well as constructivism, without adopting the orthodoxy of the former or the relativism of the latter, and should thus offer a sound foundation for relevant local government research. The characteristic features of the field invite *realistic theory construction* along the lines suggested by Pawson and Tilly (1997) in their conceptualisation of "realistic evaluation". Realistic theory construction means paying close attention to *the local contexts* of institutional or policy choices under study while seeking to identify the features of those contexts that may explain variations in institutional or policy outcomes – the search for the explanan being, of course, the essence of theory construction (Lave and March 1975, 1995).

Second, a full utilisation of the advantages of *the local government laboratory* requires that research includes a greater variety of local and national contexts by seeking to cover more countries than before in comparative research. Particular emphasis should be put on including 3rd

world countries in such research efforts. Such a programme should help addressing the paradox mentioned in the preceding section. The reviews of developments in local government around the world have yielded two somewhat contradictory impressions: on the one hand, accounts are given of tremendous changes, driven in particular by the forces of globalisation. On the other hand, the reports coming from many countries are ones of stability if not down-right inertia in local government institutions. The direction of research we advocate is seeking to understand how change is shaped by, or hindered by, a combination of local contexts and external pressures *with the aim of identifying the space for strategies that may be pursued by local actors.* The latter statement is both a plea for a focus on actors in local government research and also a commitment to produce research that may be of relevance to those actors.

Third, such an ambition necessitates attention to *cultural factors* both in institutional and policy-oriented research. Above, impacts of some factors of a cultural nature have been pointed out. What is lacking is a systematic point of departure for mapping and analysing cultural phenomena as they shape local politics and institution-building. Neo-institutional theory opens up a space for including culture as a formative element through "the logic of appropriateness" (March and Olsen 1989; 1995); at present, however, this formulation is of such a general nature that it does not help much in capturing the actual *variations* across countries and continents. Several building blocks are available for such a theory, for example concepts highlighting different attitudes to power and co-operation around the world suggested by Gert Hofstede (1997) or variations "in attitudes toward the political system and its various parts, and attitudes towards the role of the self in the system", in the formulation of Almond and Verba (1963: 13). Recently, Robert Putnam has re-launched the concept of social capital as a means to capture the significance of variations in social trust (Putnam 1993; 1999).

Fourth, in scholarly attention, *identity issues* have moved to the forefront in accounts of the grand conflicts of the day, as in the formulation of "clashes of civilizations" (Huntington 1995; 2004), replacing the theories of imperialism and global centre-periphery models that were fashionable in the 1960s and 1970s (Frank 1971). It could be argued that politics of identity are more clearly and convincingly present in institutional and policy responses at local levels of government. People increasingly demand recognition and rights based on *who they are* (or more precisely, who they *think* they are) rather than based on class or other material interests. Advocacy of gay rights, women's rights, linguistic rights or regional or ethnic distinctions have moved higher on the political agenda in many countries. The post-materialism thesis (Inglehart 1990) may go some way towards explaining such claims in the richer part of the world but can hardly account for the resurgence of identity politics in the poorer parts or in backward regions of many European countries. Identity politics tests severely the robustness and integrative capacity of existing urban and regional institutions (cf. for example the French debate on the wearing of the *hijab* in public schools). Even in a country such as the USA, with pronounced pluralistic traditions, gay marriages for example, have proved to be deeply divisive; mayors who marry gays have been stopped by their state governors, while the moral majority is in favour of constitutional amendments against such practices.

Fifth, the relationship between *policy choices* and *institutional choices* remains somewhat under-focused in the discipline. In American research, scholars for a long period claimed to see firm evidence for a link between choice of city charter and policy output. The strong-mayor model was believed to favour working class interests and mildly redistributive policies while being open to patronage and machine politics, while the manager-council plan was believed to promote professionalism and policies favoured more by the middle class (Banfield and Wilson 1963; Knoke 1981). At a later stage, more rigorous, statistical research seemed to disprove the existence of such a link (Clark 1974). It may be time to pick up this thread again in a wider context.

Sixth, processes of *globalisation* and their local impacts are emerging as a joint challenge to cities around the world; similarly, understanding these processes demands joint programmes of research and theoretical reflection that cover a multitude and variety of localities. The more extended efforts in comparative research suggested above could well be directed at understanding institutional and policy implications of globalisation. Such efforts would have to be directed at identifying the linkages and carriers of globalisation, i e how the processes is brought to bear in localities, as well as the impacts on and responses of cities. The literature is still somewhat nebulous as to the precise nature of linkages of the global and the local. As regards city responses, the literature on urban regimes may be a good place to start from when building theoretical models of configurations of policies and institutional features (Stone 1989; Stoker 1995). For example, the spread of local presidentialism may be investigated as an institutional response to new policy requirements driven by globalisation.

Seventh, despite cultural contrasts and institutional path dependencies countries and municipalities *learn* from each other across national borders and continental divides. Obviously, some municipalities are faster learners than others. Pressures of globalisation and electronic channels of communication, especially the Internet, may have speeded up cross-border learning. Understanding *the processes of learning and adaptation* in an international setting may help scholarly understanding of how globalisation impacts on local government. Municipalities have formed international arenas, networks and partnerships that provide important sources of policy learning, guidelines for institutional reconstruction and assistance in daily problem-solving. Yet these arrangements remain under-researched.

Finally, we wish to make a plea for giving more attention to *ethical issues* raised by research programmes in local government and politics. We do not make this plea because we think the subfield is more haunted by ethical difficulties than any other field of social investigation. However, in the subfield ethical issues of a special nature may be encountered. Political research is, of course, subjected to the general norms of scientific endeavour: objectivity, inter-subjectivity, and integrity. Because of the nature of their subject matter – politics – political scientists are under a special obligation to respect norms of objectivity. The issues of research are often entangled in the political front lines of the day. The ethical challenges are not limited to situations in which researchers accept research contracts funded by town halls or national agencies, and where the "problem owners" are expected to exercise some (limited) influence over the direction of research. The problem is confounded by the personal motivation of many political scientists as researchers, and in particular students of local government and politics: the wish to promote "good ends", in Robert Dahl's terms quoted above. We have suggested that "relevance" is one of the central guidelines of research in our particular sub-field. Laudable as such a motive is it may also necessitate certain precautions. The immediacy of the issues of local government addressed by scholars of the field facilitates *realism* of problem formulation but also *involvement* of researchers in problem solution. As indicated above, the realism of problem formulation is one of the strengths of the sub-field, the parallel involvement in the production of solutions requires reflection, however. We do not wish to discourage the involvement of scholars in practical issues of the day. We wish to argue the need for a *reflective framework* for the pursuit of "good ends" in ways that do not compromise the scholarly standards of the community of research. The development of such a framework should be high on the agenda of the international community of scholars engaged in studies on local government and politics. In our view, the core issue on an ethical agenda must include, in addition to attention to the canons of scholarly inquiry, a code of conduct for the interaction with stakeholders of the research programmes in which students of local government are involved[4]. For scholars working in a political context such as city politics those stakeholders will often include the immediate political and administrative environment (political leaders, council members, key administrative personnel, etc.). However, the general public and the community at large should also be seen as stakeholders of any research programme. For the community to become a real stakeholder, *openness* about procedures and

---

4   Our discussion of an ethical code is inspired in particular by that of the American Evaluation Association; cf. American Evaluation Association: Guiding Principles for Evaluators. We found the parallel code of the American Political Science Association to be somewhat vaguer regarding the issues of particular interest here, however. Surprisingly, we have not been able to identify ethical codes adopted by the IPSA or the ECPR.

results is required. Openness is, of course, always a commendable guideline for scholars. It is of particular importance in situations in which the topics of research are entangled with political positions. Control over or privileged access to information is an important political resource. *Mandatory* transparency with regard to procedures and results may work as a mechanism safeguarding objectivity and quality of research. Transparency is both deterrence against too blatant interference from "city fathers", and also opens up windows for peer checks on research methods and procedures, helping both objectivity and quality. We do not suggest that "mandatory" transparency is to be imposed through legislative action, of course. We do believe, however, that voluntarily accepted and publicly announced guidelines will have a similar effect.

References

Almond, G.A./Verba, S. (1963): *The Civic Culture. Political Attitudes and Democracy in Five Nations*. Princeton: Princeton University Press.
Bäck, H./Gjelstrup, G./Helgesen, M./Johansson, F./Klausen, JU. E. (2005): *Urban Political Decentralisation. Six Scandinavian Cities*. Wiesbaden: VS Verlag für Sozialwissenschaften. Urban and Regional Research International, vol. 5.
Baldersheim, H./Illner, M./Wollmann, H. (eds.) (2003): *Local Democracy in Post-Communist Europe*. Opladen: Leske + Budrich. Urban Research International, vol. 2.
Banfield, E.C./Wilson, J.C. (1963): *City Politics*. New York: Vintage.
Boyne, G. (1985): "Theory, Methodology and Results in Political Science – the Case of Output Studies", *British Journal of Political Science*, 15: 473-515.
Boyne, G. (1996): Constraints, Choices and Public Policies. London: JAI Press.
Cameron, R. (forthcoming): "Local Government Reform in South Africa". In: Lazin, F./Evans, M./Hoffmann-Martinot, V./Wollmann, H. (eds.): *Local Government Reforms in Countries in Transition: A Global Perspective*. Lanham: Lexington Press
Caulfield, J. (forthcoming): "Local Government Reform With Chinese Characteristics". In: Lazin, F./Evans, M./Hoffmann-Martinot, V./Wollmann, H. (eds.): *Local Government Reforms in Countries in Transition: A Global Perspective*. Lanham: Lexington Press
Clark, T.N. (1974): "Community Structure, Decision-Making, Budget Expenditure and Urban Renewal in 51 American Communities". In: Hawley, W.D./Wirt, F. M. (eds.): *The Search for Community Power*. New Jersey: Prentice-Hall.
Clark, T.N./Ferguson, L.C. (1983): *City Money, Political Processes and Retrenchment*. New York: Columbia University Press.
Cockburn, C. (1977): *The Local State. Management of Cities and People*. London: Pluto Press.
Council of Europe (2000): *Participation of Citizens in Local Political Life*. Series Local and Regional Authorities in Europe, No. 72. Strasbourg: Council of Europe Publishing.

Dahl, R. et al. (2004): "What have We Learned?" Chapter 17. In: Shapiro, I./Smith, R.M./Masoud, T.E. (2004): *Problems and Methods in the Study of Politics.* Cambridge: Cambridge University Press.

Denters, B./Rose, L.E. (2005): "Towards Local Governance?" In: Denters, B./Rose, L.E. (eds.): *Comparing Local Governance. Trends and Developments.* London: Palgrave.

Denters, B./Rose, L.E. (eds.) (2005): *Comparing Local Governance. Trends and Developments.* London: Palgrave.

Frank, A.G. (1971): *Capitalism and Underdevelopment in Latin America.* Hammondsworth: Penguin Books.

Harriss, J./Stokke, K./Törnquist, O. (eds.) (2004): *Politicising Democracy. The New Local Politics of Democratisation.* London: Palgrave.

Hoeber R.S. et al. (2004): "What Have We Learned?" Chapter 17. In: Hapiro, I./ Smith, R.M./Masoud, T.E. (2004): *Problems and Methods in the Study of Politics.* Cambridge: Cambridge University Press.

Hofstede, G. (1997): *Cultures and Organizations: Software of the Mind.* New York: McGraw-Hill. Rev. ed.

Huntington, S.P. (1996): The *Clash of Civilizations and the Remaking of World Order.* New York: Simon & Schuster.

Jamil, I. (1999): *Administrative Culture in Bangladesh.* Bergen: University of Bergen. Ph. D. Thesis.

John, P. (2001): *Local Goverance in Western Europe,* London: Sage.

Kahn, M.M./Obaidullah, A.T.M. (2003): "Local Government in Bangladesh: Evolution, Reorganization, Centre-Local Relations and Critical Issues". In: Vajpeyi, D. (ed.) (2003): *Local Democracy and Politics in South Asia.* Opladen: Leske + Budrich. Urban Research International, vol. 3.

Knoke, D. (1981): Urban Political Cultures. In: Clark, T.N. (ed.): *Urban Policy Analysis.Directions for Future Research.* Beverly Hills: Sage. Vol. 21, Urban Affairs Annual Review

Kundera, M. (1984): "The Tragedy of Central Europe", *New York Review of Books,* 26 April 1984.

Lave, C.A./March, J.G. (1975/1993): *An introduction to models in the social sciences.* New York: Harper & Row (2nd ed. Lanham, Md.: University Press of America, 1993).

Pawson, R./Tilly, N. (1997): *Realistic Evaluation.* London: Sage.

Lakatos, I. (1970): "Falsification and the Methodology of Scientific Research Programmes". In: Lakatos, I./Musgrave, A. (eds.): *Criticism and the Growth of Knowledge.* Cambridge: Cambridge University Press.

Lasswell, H.D.: "The Policy Orientation", In: Lerner, D./Lasswell, H.D. (eds.): *The Policy Sciences.* Stanford: Stanford University Press.

Lodge, T. (2002): Politics in South Africa. From Mandela to Mbeki. Cape Town: David Philip.

Logan, J.R./Moltoch, H.L. (1987): *Urban Fortunes: The Political Economy of Place.* Berkeley: University of California Press.

March, J.G./Olsen, J.P. (1989): *Rediscovering Institutions. The Organizational Basis of Politics.* London: Collier Macmillan.

Nakamura, A. (2002): "A Paradigm Shift in Japan's Intergovernmental Relations: Reform of Government and Dencentralization of Central Power", In: Caulfield,

J./Larsen, H.O. (eds.): *Local Government at the Millennium*. Opladen: Leske + Budrich Urban Research International Series 1.

Oberst, R. (2003): "Dencentralization and Local Politics in Sri Lanka", In: Vajpeyi, D. (ed.) (2003): *Local Democracy and Politics in South Asia*. Opladen: Leske + Budrich. Urban Research International 3.

Olowu, D. (1995): "The African Experience in Local Government", In: Reddy, P.S. (ed.): *Perspectives on Local Government, Management and Development in Africa*. Durban: Department of Public Administration, University of Durban-Westville.

Peters, B.G. (1999): *Institutional Theory in Political Science*. Continuum International Publishing Group.

Peterson, P.E. (1980): *City Limits*. Chicago: University of Chicago Press.

Pollitt, C./Bouckaert, G. (2000) : *Public Management Reform. A Comparative Analysis*. Oxford: Oxford University Press.

Ingelhart, R. (1990): *Cultural Shift in Advanced Industrial Society*. Princeton: Princeton University Press.

Rhodes, R.A.W. (1997) : Understanding Governance. Policy Networks, Governance, Reflexibility and Accountability. Buckingham: Open University Press.

Sancton, A. (2002): "Local Government in North America: Localism and Community Governance", In: Caulfield, J./Larsen, H.O. (eds.): *Local Government at the Millennium*. Opladen: Leske + Budrich Urban Research International Series 1.

Savitch, H.V./Vogel, R.K. (2005): "The United States: Executive-Centred Politics", Chapter 13. In: Denters, B./Rose, L.E. (eds.): *Comparing Local Governance. Trends and Developments*. London: Palgrave.

Schöpflin, G./Wood, N. (eds.) (1989): *In Search of Central Europe*. Oxford: Polity Press.

Seton-Watson, H. (1989): "What is Europe? Where is Europe? From Mystique to Politique", Chapter 2. In: Schöpflin, G./Wood, N. (eds.) (1989): *In Search of Central Europe*. Oxford: Polity Press. Originally printed in *Encounter*, vol. 65, No. 2.

Shapiro, I./Smith, R.M./Masoud, T.E. (2004): "Introduction: Problems and Methods in the Study of Politics", Chapter 1. In: Shapiro, I./Smith, R.M./Masoud, T.E. (2004): *Problems and Methods in the Study of Politics*. Cambridge: Cambridge University Press.

Shapiro, I./Smith, R.M./Masoud, T.E. (2004): *Problems and Methods in the Study of Politics*. Cambridge: Cambridge University Press.

Stoker, G. (1990): "Regulation Theory, Local Government and the Transition from Fordism', In: King, D.E./Pierre, J. (eds.): *Theories of Urban Politics*. London: Sage.

Stoker, G. (1995): "Regime Theory and Urban Politics", In: Judge, D./Stoker, G./ Wollmann, H. (eds.): *Theories of Urban Politics*. London: Sage

Stoker, G. (2004): *Transforming Local Governance. From Thatcherism to New Labour*. Houndsmill: Palgrave. Government Beyond the Centre Series.

Stone, C. (1989): *Regime Politics. Governing Atlanta 1946-1988*. Lawrence: University of Alabama Press.

Sullivan, H. (2003): "Local Government Reform in Great Britain". In: Kersting, N./ Vetter, A. (eds.) (2003): *Reforming Local Government in Europe. Closing the*

Gap Between Democracy and Efficiency. Opladen: Leske + Buridch. Urban Research International, vol. 4.

Vajpeyi, D./Arnold, J.M. (2003): "Evolution of Local Self-Government in India", In: Vajpeyi, D. (ed.) (2003): *Local Democracy and Politics in South Asia.* Opladen: Leske + Budrich. Urban Research International, vol. 3.

Vajpeyi, D. (ed.) (2003): "Pakistan: Experiments in Local Governance", In: Vajpeyi, D. (ed.) (2003): *Local Democracy and Politics in South Asia.* Opladen: Leske + Budrich. Urban Research International, vol. 3.

Vajpeyi, D. (ed.) (2003): *Local Democracy and Politics in South Asia.* Opladen: Leske + Budrich. Urban Research International, vol. 3.

Vanags, E./Vilka, I. (2003): "Local Democracy in the Baltic Countries: A New Beginning?" In: Baldersheim, H./Illner, M./Wollmann, H. (eds.): *Local Democracy in Post-Communist Europe.* Opladen: Leske + Budrich. Urban Research International Series, vol. 2.

Wollmann, H. (2003): "Policy Knowledge and Contractual Research", in *International Encyclopedia of Social and Behavioral Sciences.* Vol. 5. Amsterdam: Elsevier

Wollmann, H./Butusova, N. (2003): "Local Self-Government in Russia: Precarious Trajectory Between Power and Law", In: Baldersheim, H./Illner, M./Wollmann, H. (eds.): *Local Democracy in Post-Communist Europe.* Opladen: Leske + Budrich. Urban Research International Series, vol. 2.

Wollmann, H. (2005): "Applied Social Science Developments, State of the Art, Consequences", In: UNESCO ed. *History of Humanity,* Vol. VII, Chapter 21. London: Routledge.

About the contributors

Harald Baldersheim is professor of public administration at the Department of Political Science, University of Oslo.
http://www.statsvitenskap.uio.no/ansatte/presentasjon/vit/eng/haraldba.html

Susan E. Clarke is Professor of Political Science and Director of the Center to Advance Research and Teaching in the Social Sciences (CARTSS) at the University of Colorado at Boulder.
http://cartss.colorado.edu/

Michael Goldsmith is Emeritus Professor of Politics and Government at the University of Salford, UK and Visiting Professor at FNSP, Paris.

Vincent Hoffmann-Martinot is CNRS research director at the CERVL Pouvoir Action Publique Territoire/Sciences Po Bordeaux.
http://www.cervl.sciencespobordeaux.fr/PagesCV/Hoffmann-Martinot.htm

Peter John is the Hallsworth Chair of Governance at the University of Manchester, UK.
http://www.ipeg.org.uk/about/john.htm

Hellmut Wollmann is professor (emeritus) of public policy and public administration at Humboldt University Berlin.

Index

India 24, 29, 117, 121, 131
infrastructure of research 83
institutional thickness 45
intergovernmental relations 11, 16-17, 104
intermediate tier 14, 21

J
Japan 87-88, 91, 114, 120, 129

M
Marxist 15, 24, 28-29, 71, 120
meso level 11, 21, 115
methods- and theory-driven studies 122
metropolitan government 11, 13, 113
Mie Prefecture 114
mobilisation of bias 12
multi-level governance 22, 37, 39, 44
multinomial probit 70

N
Nepal 117
networks 17, 23, 37-38, 40, 42, 44-45, 68, 72, 75-76, 79-80, 83, 92, 126
new information technologies 33-34, 40
New Labour 112, 123, 130
new political culture 12, 47-48, 120
New Public Management 18-20, 28, 111, 121
new regionalism 39-40
New Zealand 18, 111
Nigerian 116
Norway 13, 19, 29-30, 77, 79-81, 100, 112
numerosity 68, 73, 78, 110, 123

O
output studies 11, 14, 25, 70

P
Pakistan 117-118, 131
participation 11, 19-20, 41, 45, 51-53, 55-56, 61, 77, 79-81, 85, 94, 100, 117
partnerships 18, 45, 54, 86, 113, 126
path dependency 23-24, 113-114
performance 20-21, 51, 68-69, 74, 78, 86, 114, 117
performance coalition 51

performance regimes 51
policy 12, 14, 16-17, 21, 23, 33-34, 39-40, 42-45, 47, 49-51, 54-56, 59, 63, 67, 69, 73-74, 76-80, 87, 95, 101, 104-107, 109, 114, 117, 119-126, 133
policy choices 42, 44, 45, 49-50, 119, 123-124, 126
policy communities 17, 120
policy sciences 122, 124
political incorporation 47, 52-53, 55-57
Portugal 17, 112
post-communist countries 10, 112, 114
post-Fordist 40
power 12, 15, 24, 34-35, 38, 40, 42, 46, 50, 53, 57, 67, 72, 75-76, 90, 102, 109, 111, 113, 115-116, 125
privatization 20
problem-driven research 122-123
propinquity 68, 71-73, 78, 110, 123
public choice 20
public private partnerships 45

Q
Qualitative Comparative Analysis 74, 80
quasi-experiment 74

R
realist scientificism 124
realistic evaluation 124
regime theory 11, 22, 41-42, 45, 71
regression techniques 70
regulation theory 24, 120
rescaling 34, 38-39
Russia 88, 115-116, 119, 131

S
social capital 11-12, 19-20, 68, 125
social exclusion/cohesion 52, 54-55
social movements 15, 37
South Africa 91, 101, 116, 119, 121, 128-129
South Asia 117-118, 121, 129-131
Soviet Union 116
Sri Lanka 117-118, 130
street-level bureaucrats 73
subsidiarity 21
Sweden 13, 16, 20, 26, 54, 77, 102, 106, 111

The World of Political Science – The Development of the Discipline Book Series Edited by Michael Stein and John Trent

The book series aims at going beyond the traditional "state-of-the-art review" and wants to make a major contribution not just to the description of the state of the discipline, but also to an explanation of its development and content.

Linda Shepherd (ed.)
Political Psychology
2006. 168 pp. Pb.
19.90 €/ US$ 23.95
ISBN 3-86649-027-5

The book provides detailed information about the development of the field of political psychology, a subfield of both political science and psychology. It describes the evolution of concepts and theories within political psychology, international influences in the field, current concepts and methodology, and trends that augur for the future of the enterprise.

R.B. Jain (ed.)
Governing development
across cultures
Challenges and dilemmas of an emerging
sub-discipline in political science
2006. Approx. 200 pp. Pb
Approx. 19.90 €/ US$ 23.95
ISBN 3-96649-029-1

The book is a critical examination and appraisal of the status, methodology and likely future of the emerging sub-discipline of "Governing Development" within the broader discipline of political science.

David Coen & Wyn Grant (eds.)
Business and Government
Methods and Practice
2006. 127 pp. Pb. 16.90 €/ US$ 19.90
ISBN 3-86649-033-X

This volume reviews current debates on the role of business in politics and it assesses emerging methodological approaches to its study.

Verlag Barbara Budrich
Barbara Budrich Publishers

Head-office: Stauffenbergstr. 7 • D-51379 Leverkusen Opladen • Germany
Tel +49 (0)2171.344.594 • Fax +49 (0)2171.344.693 • info@budrich-verlag.de
US-office: 28347 Ridgebrook • Farmington Hills, MI 48334 • USA • info@barbara-budrich.net
Northamerican distribution: International Specialized Book Services
920 NE 58th Ave., suite 300 • Portland, OR 97213-3786 • USA
phone toll-free within North America 1-800-944-6190, fax 1-503-280-8832 •orders@isbs.com

www.budrich-verlag.de • **www.barbara-budrich.net**